COMING
HOME
FROM
DEVIL
MOUNTAIN

COMING HOME FROM DEVIL MOUNTAIN

Eleanor Dart O'Bryon

HARBINGER HOUSE

TUCSON

Harbinger House, Inc.
Tucson, Arizona
© 1989 by Eleanor Dart O'Bryon
All Rights Reserved
Manufactured in the United States of America
This book was set in 11/13 Granjon

Library of Congress Cataloging in Publication Data

O'Bryon, Eleanor Dart, 1946–
    Coming home from Devil Mountain / Eleanor Dart O'Bryon.
        p.   cm.
    ISBN 0-943173-20-5
    1. O'Bryon, Eleanor Dart. 1946–   . 2. Mountaineers—United States—
Biography.   3. Mountaineering—Mexico—Cerro de la Encantada—Search and
rescue operations.   4. Fathers and daughters—United States—Case studies.   I. Title.
GV199.92.037A3   1989   796.5′22′092—dc20   [B]   89-15573

For Francis Elliot Dart, my father.

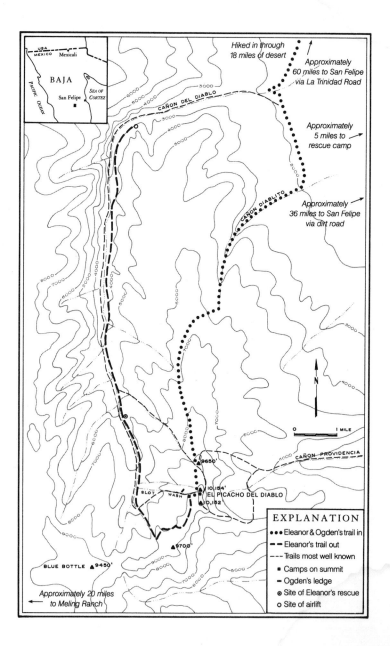

Hiked in through
18 miles of desert

Approximately
60 miles to San Felipe
via La Trinidad Road

Approximately
5 miles to
rescue camp

Approximately
36 miles to San Felipe
via dirt road

CAÑON DEL DIABLO

CAÑON DIABLITO

BAJA

USA
MEXICO   Mexicali

PACIFIC OCEAN

San Felipe

SEA OF CORTEZ

N

O   1 MILE

CAÑON PROVIDENCIA

9650'

SLOT   WASH

10,154' EL PICACHO DEL DIABLO
10,152'

9700'

BLUE BOTTLE 9450'

Approximately 20 miles
to Meling Ranch

EXPLANATION

••• Eleanor & Ogden's trail in
– – – Eleanor's trail out
- - - Trails most well known
■ Camps on summit
– Ogden's ledge
⊚ Site of Eleanor's rescue
○ Site of airlift

CONTENTS

In the spring of 1967 at the age of twenty I was lost in the mountains in Baja, Mexico. My father was there too, searching for me. Reunited at length and sharing the journals we had both kept, we made a promise to each other that someday we would publish our story. This book is the fulfillment of that promise. Our journals are included here in their entirety, just as we wrote them. This also is a story of internal search over twenty years' time, and of a journey that is not over yet.

Eleanor Dart O'Bryon

ACKNOWLEDGMENTS

I wish to thank Alan Harrington and Charles Bowden for their unfailing kindness and generous help. Each read the manuscript numerous times in its several versions. With painstaking attention to detail and thoughtful criticism Alan lent me his years of experience in seeing a book through from first idea to final printing. By saying just enough and no more Chuck helped me to face hard truths and write about them honestly.

COMING
HOME
FROM
DEVIL
MOUNTAIN

1

Ripples on the Surface

It is night. I am alone in a strange house in La Jolla. Ogden is in the hospital. The bedroom has blue ruffled curtains. A nightlight glows. Everything is clean and silent. I am frightened and I wander through empty rooms looking for comfort. Behind two giant red-lacquered doors I find a thin woman sleeping in a big round bed. I am crying. She puts on a green silk robe, fusses me back to bed, gives me tranquilizers. The pills send me downward into dizzying spirals of blackness that increase in velocity when I close my eyes. I cannot sleep.

The next morning I am next door at Ogden's grandparents' house sitting alone at the dining room table. A maid in a black uniform with a starched white apron sets a plate holding a poached egg on toast in front of me. I burst into tears.

Back in Claremont I feel safe in the familiar clutter and smells of my Uncle Leonard's home. My mother is here. She pours her heart into cooking five small perfect meals each day, which she brings to the darkened bedroom on a tray. I can rest at last, only I can't seem to rest. My father arrives and we spend a night sitting on the bed together talking. Some current moving through us joins as we share our stories. I need him, I need to touch him, to tell him . . . what? Something has happened to me that I do not understand and it is more important to me than Mother or food or Ogden. I sense that my father feels it too—he is a lifeline and I hold on. Then he is gone to Thailand.

Many people want to talk to me. A preacher friend of the family gives a sermon entitled "It's in Your Hands Now," and sends me a copy with a drawing of a man sprawled on a rock ledge and a woman on the ledge below him raising her arms to the sky. Words like "God" and "miracle" and "faith" are ripples on the surface all around me. Someone tells me it is April—I have lost track of the days. I know I am in a state of grace but cannot explain what this means to anyone, not even to myself.

There is no question of returning to school. Ogden's feet are badly frozen. I move back to Oregon into my parents' house. I tell my old friends what I can about the mountain, and they are always very moved. I become really good at this. Everyone seems to be sure Ogden and I will marry and devote our lives to paying back our debt to the world.

Now it is July and I have walked up into the hills behind our house, where I have gone since childhood when I need time alone. I sit beneath Douglas firs, looking out over the rolling green lawns and quiet neighborhoods of west Eugene. I am trying to feel. I cannot feel anything. I am numb, empty.

A small plane flies over, I hear the engine and suddenly I find myself on my feet waving my arms, screaming "Help! Help!" I do not climb another mountain for twenty years.

2

Daughter of a Quaker Saint

"The Mexicans call it 'The Devil's Peak' and perhaps there is good reason. . . ."

Ogden is reading me an article torn from *Desert* magazine. The pages are crumpled and dirty from being carried in his pocket with his ragged copy of Kerouac's *The Dharma Bums*. It is my second year at Pitzer College in Claremont, California. Ogden Kellogg and I are living together off campus. Spring vacation is coming and Ogden wants to climb "El Picacho del Diablo." He asks me if I will go with him.

Ogden is tall and long-limbed, with a tumble of dark hair, liquid brown eyes and a shy, embarrassed smile. He is a pacifist, a romantic dreamer studying Chinese language and pottery. A week after we met I joined him to hitchhike home for Christmas.

The trip was a revelation. My restlessness, the longing I seemed to have felt all my life to break out, just to GO . . . all found a focus on the road. No car, no money, no permission . . . you just stroll down to the nearest highway, stick out your thumb and you're gone. I was dizzy with freedom. But when I walked up the driveway with my bus money still in hand, my father was furious.

My father is a physicist and a Quaker. He teaches at the University of Oregon when he is not traveling in Asia. Foreign governments who wish to develop their own research scientists hire my father. He is a patient man and a good listener. He walks on dirt paths into remote villages in Nepal, Thailand, Australia, New Guinea. He sits on the ground, drinking tea, and talks with the elders about how the world was made, about lightning and thunder and the sources of knowledge. He asks children to draw him maps and tell him stories. Then he designs grade school curricula that help the children learn to explore the world with their hands and eyes, as well as through the chants of the shamans.

At home in Oregon my father loves to fish for trout in the high mountain lakes. He spends days standing on the ends of dry snags, or floating in a tiny yellow raft he packs in on his back, trailing wet flies through the green water. He always catches fish—bright rainbows and speckled browns. When I go with him we roll the trout in cornmeal, cook them in an iron frying pan and eat sitting on soft banks of pine needles, separating the tender pink flesh from the tiny bones.

The summer before I started college my father and I backpacked together into the Kalalau Valley on the island of Kauai. We climbed steep trails above a turquoise ocean and met native hunters who gave us a leg of wild goat, which we cooked with chunks of green papaya into a pungent stew. In the Kalalau we found the abandoned taro fields and shrines of a lost civilization. We played in surf that surged into deep caverns above the beach and bathed in waterfalls. At night as we lay in our sleepings bags Daddy told me about falling in love with my mother, about working with refugees in post-war Germany, about growing up in Africa. We had never been so close.

My father has a firm mouth and clear blue eyes with a direct searching gaze. When he laughs his eyes sparkle and soften, but he is more often stern. He gives an impression always of complete integrity.

That Christmas he looked at me standing before him, defiant in my hiking boots and knapsack. A true Quaker, he controlled his anger. His refusal to blow up made the disapproval in his voice even more intense.

"You're old enough to make your own decisions," he said. "But I don't like this one."

Back at college January seems to last forever—the days and nights merge into a swirling blackness. It is 1967. Vietnam beats against our minds. A young Quaker burns himself alive on the steps of the Pentagon. Classified 1-A and sure to be drafted, Ogden is desperate. At night he packs for Canada while I sit out in the dark yard crying. The next day he decides to stay, refuse military service, go to jail. He dreams of making some grand sacrificial gesture but lacks the courage. In my classes the professors teach on, apparently unaware that the world is cracking apart.

Now Ogden and I are sitting on the green college lawn in weak winter sunlight. He is telling me about the mountain in Mexico. This mountain has caught his imagination . . . it is some sort of quest, a personal pilgrimage he must make. I barely listen. An adventure . . . an escape to the simplicity of rocks and sweat . . . of course I will go.

◆

The northeastern coast of the Sea of Cortez, which lies between the Baja Peninsula and mainland Mexico, is one of the driest deserts in the world. No rivers reach the sea from this shore of sand and rock. Legend has it that in the sixteenth century coasting Spanish sailors saw across the water to the west the snowcapped peak of a great mountain. "La Providencia" they called it, God's gift of moisture to a burning land.

This highest peak in Baja is named "Cerro de la Encantada" (Mountain of Enchantment) on Mexican maps. "El Picacho del Diablo" say the local peasants and ranchers who know her better. Rising almost two miles into the sky from the desert at its eastern base, the mountain is a jumbled mass of white granite boulders and vertical cliffs, cut by steep canyons, crowned by a chain of summits. At the base El Diablo stretches over fifteen miles from north to south. Seen from San Felipe, a small fishing village on the Sea of Cortez, it appears to be a mountain range rather than a single peak.

West of El Picacho a deep gorge known as Cañon Diablo lies between the mountain and the Sierra San Pedro Martir, one of the central fault blocks that form the backbone of the Baja Peninsula. At the head of Diablo Canyon the mountain's southernmost summit is connected by a knifelike ridge to Blue Bottle, a smaller peak on the Sierra.

Facing El Picacho across Diablo canyon is the Sierra's eastern escarpment, seventy-five miles of cliffs dropping 6,000–8,000 feet to the desert bordering the Sea of Cortez. On the west the Sierra descends gently toward the Pacific as a sloping plateau, covered by pine forests and open meadows. No villages are to be found on this tableland, and few year-round streams, but a handful of Mexican ranchers run cattle there, and thirty-five miles to the northwest is the large Rancho San Jose, a cattle and guest ranch owned by Salvador Meling.

Early climbers of Picacho Diablo almost without exception underestimated the mountain's obstacles. Accounts of ascents in the 1930s and '50s are stories of overnight attempts that stretched into days, unplanned bivouacs without food or shelter, running out of water and retreat in the face of weather. Between 1911 and 1951 four parties reached the 10,154-foot south summit, each by a different route.

In 1955 a party led by Bud Bernhard ascended the twenty-mile-long L-shaped Cañon Diablo and roped up a gully Bernhard named "Cold Slot Wash" to the summit. This became the standard route for future climbs, usually taking four days.

◆

5:00 A.M. Dawn is a gray whisper in the blackness as I pack for the trip. My harmonica, boots and a rope, a paperback edition of the works of Walt Whitman, Ogden's pocket-sized game of *go*, four days worth of brown rice, oatmeal and raisins for the climb. And a small black book with "Record" embossed on the cover in gold—my journal.

3

The Road to El Picacho

From the Journal of Eleanor Dart, 1967

We hitched out of Claremont today, the first day of spring vacation. Caught a quick ride to Riverside where we stopped at a mountaineering store and bought a pale blue parka for Ogden, some soap, lemonade. Ogden's roommate Gordon Bailey met us there. He looked at me in my flowered dress and army surplus hat (forty-nine cents) and said I was like one of the Victorian lady explorers who set out to walk across Africa in long black dresses carrying parasols.

Rode on Gordon's motorcycle to the edge of town. Uh oh, two hitchhikers already there, a man and his girl with packs, the girl sitting disconsolately on the ground next to a guitar, hugging her sleeping bag.

"Been here long?"

"It's a slow place; about forty-five minutes."

They'd just gotten a ticket for hitching the freeway. We decided to try the next exit.

Sunny afternoon—Ogden leaned against the "No Pedestrians" sign by the freeway, tall and loose in his white shirt against the blue sky.

We soon caught a ride with a white driver and an old black man with lisping, hesitant speech. Crossed the Elsinore fault—small, steep hills eroded by stream gullies and overgrown with sagebrush. Between them we caught glimpses of the snow-tipped peaks of the San Bernardino Mountains.

We climbed out at a cold, windy exit and immediately got a ride with an old man carrying sacks of feed for the quail on his place. Stopped at a farmer's market and went nuts looking at grapefruit, bread, oranges, dates—I was so hungry. We bought a small jar of mountain sage honey and a bag of macaroons.

Dropped off at dusk on a deserted stretch of road, we hiked across the barriers to hitch the freeway. A rattle-trap jeep pulled up and we ran to climb in, Ogden's pale blue parka gleaming in the dusk.

The driver was a wild old man named Joe. Tanned, seamed face, ancient hat, kept adjusting his teeth. Southern accent. Told him we were going to the Salton Sea . . . planned to camp there overnight.

"No kidding!" By golly, he was camped on the Salton Sea himself. Squatting in a little pasteboard shack that nobody owned. Had water, firewood, grapefruit orchard right behind him . . . "pick as much grapefruit as you want." We stopped at a Safeway to buy fish for his kitten, a pure white kitten. . . .

"Bet you five dollars she meets us on the road."

Stopped for coffee, drove on, stopped for water, then down a rutted dirt road. On one side Indian land, completely undeveloped, the other side planted in some crop—sugarcane, or corn.

KLUNK! One muffler fell off and dragged noisily behind. On into the dark under a million stars . . . there . . . a white kitten appeared out of the blackness and led us over a hill into a squatter's paradise.

Pasteboard shack—inside the narrow door a cooking place,

shelves, clothing boxes, a narrow bed—tiny, dark, dirty. Outside—two trees with a board table nailed between them and three wicker chairs. A coal oil lantern casts a soft pool of light.

We built a fire and cooked soup and steaks, feasted on Joe's bread, peanut butter and jam and coffee. We sat under the stars and talked late about people, places, Carlsbad Cavern. . . .

"I'm telling you that is the grandest sight you'll ever see. Caves big enough to seat 3,000. Jeweled caverns like diamonds. You see an Indian woman holding a baby, big as life, but she's carved out of stone. And bats! You never see a sign of 'em and then at 5:00 on the nose they come pouring out so thick you can't see the other side of the cave, and they fly up and out of the top of the cavern like black smoke out of a volcano and rise so high they disappear. And they're gone 'til 5:00 comes around again and then down they come out of nowhere and disappear into the caves again. You'll never see a grander sight. It's just . . . grand!"

And so into the night.

SATURDAY, FEBRUARY 4
BY THE SALTON SEA

This morning Joe drove us out to the road after loading us with ripe grapefruit. The rides came fast—an old man, a young boy, an Esso tank-truck driver, high in the cab. Finally we ran out of luck in the small town of Brawley, and I had bad menstrual cramps, so we sat on the curb. A policeman stopped to give us the once-over. He filled in our vital statistics (home, name, age, school, major) on little white cards. Friendly . . . finally left. We soon got a ride to Calexico with a Mexican gentleman who owns a drugstore across the border in Mexicali.

A bustle of people at the border—Mexicans coming into Calexico to shop, gringos going to Mexico. We walked into the visa office with our packs and were confronted by a dark, stout official who demanded I show my birth certificate as proof of citizenship. Alas! I haven't got it. Here are my driver's license, my social security card. . . . No! They will not do. I am near tears; he is unmoved. We tramp back into Calexico to find a notary public. His secretary gives me documents saying I am a U.S. citizen and soon we are in Mexicali.

There is Carnival—a fiesta—this weekend in San Felipe, where we are headed, so we have decided to take the special bus instead of hitchhiking. We are waiting in a crowded bus station with a peasant woman wrapped in a shawl, her children and cowboy husband, and two young men who keep turning to stare at me.

A long drive—193 kilometers of mountains, cactus, salt flats, desert—only one or two houses to be seen the whole way. I slept.

San Felipe is jammed with people. A tiny fishing town with two main streets, it is usually a dusty, sleepy place. But this weekend there are stalls set up everywhere selling hats, sunglasses, tacos, serapes, roast corn . . . and dozens of small Mexican boys selling Chiclets from cardboard boxes.

We walked out onto a long sand beach to look at the blue sea and watch soldiers, very young boys in gray uniforms, strolling by the water with their girls. A cock fight was in progress under a circus tent farther down the beach. We found a small cove and hid our packs in a narrow streambed.

Dinner in town at a small empty restaurant—enchiladas and Tecate beer served by a lovely girl with a dark ponytail and a beautiful shy smile—about ten years old.

Carnival! Hot roasted corn, juicy and salty, gummy candied apples, throngs of people from Mexicali. A Mexican hippie band begins to play and young gringos—the boys barefoot and clutching beer bottles, the girls in outlandish mod-hip outfits (tight flowered pants, high boots with spats)—gyrate insanely with the jerking out-of-joint waggletail gringo dances. One Mexican couple dances sedately, sensuously, in waltz position. The residents of San Felipe form a closed silent circle around the dance floor. They watch intently, seriously. No one smiles.

A young San Felipe girl, a slender flame in red wool, dances wildly, beautifully. She tosses her dark head and laughs.

Everyone floods down the street for speeches and a fireworks display. Ogden and I walked slowly back to our cove through the darkness. We made our bed on the sand and fell asleep listening to the rush, sigh and retreat of the waves.

SUNDAY, FEBRUARY 5
SAN FELIPE

We woke early to see the sun rise over the blue sea. Cooked oatmeal with raisins and milk over a small fire. Beach explorers wandered across our cove.

We decided to build sand castles using the jagged black rocks by the water for a foundation. Ogden builds a fairy-tale castle of towering twisted drip-turrets and weird gateways. I build a solid medieval fortress with thick walls and firm round towers, surrounded by a deep moat.

A family playing on the beach watches us with amusement. Their teenage daughter talks with Ogden in Spanish; the young children begin to build sand castles too.

Lying on the warm sand with Ogden's curly dark head resting in the curve of my armpit, his long body firm against mine, I shelter his eyes from the sun.

The beach is finally free of people and Ogden strips to his shorts and runs into the water, plunging and emerging like a dolphin. The water is cold, blue-green and clear. I dive into the waves, splashing and laughing. We embrace, slippery wet bodies, and dry each other, shivering.

Afternoon. We pack our gear and walk into San Felipe for a dinner of deep-fried shrimp with tortillas. The carnival is more crowded than ever. A parade commences—two floats, one with a carnival queen, firemen marching and the Red Cross truck slowly move up the two dusty main streets and back, two times around.

At the edge of town we hitch a ride in a car with four young Mexican men decked out in festive feather hats and drinking Coronas. We crowd in and talk. They are much amused by my feeble Spanish. We climb out at El Pariso, the one restaurant between San Felipe and Mexicali. It is a small board building, desolate beside a road that vanishes into the distant mountains. The proprietors are a young man and his old grandmother. She has a wrinkled kind face, weathered, wrapped in a green wool shawl.

We wait in this lonely place, hoping for an eventual ride toward the mountains. Expecting to spend the night, we build a small fire. I buy caramels. The young man assures us that someone will come. Darkness falls and he lights three kerosene lamps, setting one on the counter. A black and white kitten comes to sit by it. Golden lamplight, soft kitten fur gleaming.

Trucks stop for salt. Farmers' trucks rattle out from the mountains, going to Mexicali with firewood. A pickup truck pulls in and stops, sitting in blackness for a while with no sign of life. The restaurant man talks to the driver. Yes, they are going inland; they have room for two more. We climb into the back and fit ourselves in with three young boys, gas tank, hose, water cans and blankets.

"But surely the young lady would prefer to ride in the cab . . . she will be cold. *Por favor*!"

"No," we assure them, I will be all right.

Cramped in, freezing wind, tangled quilts, clear icy millions of stars, pitch-black sky. We rattle off into the night. Once we stop where another pickup has gone off the road into the sand. The owners have built a fire to work by, red flames casting dark moving shadows on the road.

We drive on, colder and colder. Stop to siphon gas into the tank. The truck breaks down.

"Ohhhh! Ohhh noooo!" wails our driver. Much puttering. It starts again, goes 200 yards, stops.

"Ohhhh! Ohhh noooo!" We continue to break down. It becomes apparent that the truck will probably never make it over the mountains.

Ogden decides this is as good a place as any for us to get out, so we climb down in a whipping wind. It feels strange to walk into the desert so many miles from anywhere at night alone. Away from the road we set up our tarps in the darkness and crawl in out of the wind.

MONDAY, FEBRUARY 6
BY THE LA TRINIDAD ROAD

When I woke up the desert was bathed in translucent early morning light, framing the cactus in furry gold. Ogden was nowhere to be seen. He soon returned, having decided upon our route. We ate brown bread and honey with raisins and set off across the desert. It is twenty miles to the mountain.

The desert shines and glitters in the sun. Every kind of cactus—short round water carriers, giant many-armed skyscrapers, small little pricklers—*everything* has spines. As the day got hotter my feet began to develop bad blisters.

Noon fire. Cooked brown rice and gravy. Delicious juicy grapefruit in the shade of a low tree.

Night. We camped on a low hill covered with fortresslike granite boulders. A perfect hideout for Indians or Mexican communist revolutionaries. Fire, sunset. We talked . . . we haven't for so long. Somehow I felt separate from Ogden; he seemed distant and preoccupied. I guess he was thinking about the route and the mountain. Lying beside him I still felt alone.

Orion is with us every night.

4

Now I Am Alone

From the Journal of Eleanor Dart

I woke to Ogden's cry of "Hoo! Hoo!" from the rock above me.

As the blistering day wore on, my feet became excruciatingly painful. I slowly trudged along, keeping myself moving with marching songs: "We Are Marching to Picacho." "When Johnny Comes Marching Home Again, Hurrah, Hurrah!" "Highland Laddie."

By afternoon we reached the tremendous bouldery wash from one of the main canyons of El Picacho. Every step had become an agony. Finally I sat down and cried against Ogden's shoulder. Then I could go on. We found water. Went on to the next canyon, which seemed more likely to be Arroyo del Diablo, the main route, despite its much smaller sandy wash. I waited high on a hill while Ogden checked it out. He came back for my pack.

Winding streambeds, a corral for horses and a horse trail under shady trees. We camped on a sandy beach by a pool.

Firelight on trees. Bathed in icy water by moonlight. Refreshed, we drank hot lemonade and went to bed. I lay looking up at black leaf shapes against the dark sky.

WEDNESDAY, FEBRUARY 8

We cooked an utterly ghastly breakfast of pudding—a combination of stale brown bread, raisins, water and honey. I managed to choke most of the mess down.

Decided to hike in my moccasins, and we set off up the canyon. Some things I will never forget. . . .

The first waterfall—sheer smooth granite, maybe thirty feet high. We climbed it roped, to the right of the main fall. This must be the one a 1935 party had so much trouble with, we thought.

Later, around a bend—a giant waterfall, perhaps 360 feet, with ferns, moss, fir trees and palms growing out of the water-stained rock. Enormous smooth curves of granite at the base and a dark pool with a sandy beach. Ogden climbed the first 120 feet unroped just for fun, and I watched, afraid, as he struggled to get back down. This one we'll have to climb around. But how?

We decided on a route up the cliff to the left, across a brushy ledge and up a gendarme above the falls. Hauled our packs up the first part in an hour of dusty struggle through dense tangled brush. A low point in our hopes—we were so high up, we'd come so far—we didn't want to turn back. Finally over the gendarme and it goes.

Exhausted, we decided to camp on a sandy ledge directly above the waterfall. A weird time . . . dusk is falling . . . everything is uncertain. The canyon, its granite walls towering above us in the last pale light, seems a fearful place, haunted by strange winds, inhabited by ghosts and silent demons. We were awestruck. We felt so small, so alone, with night coming.

We gathered wood, built a fire, talked to reassure ourselves.

Slowly the tiny ledge above the giant falls ceased to be a frightening place and became homey.

You see, we both knew by now we were not in Diablo Canyon. We had chosen an unknown route. I was climbing in moccasins, forcing my blistered feet into boots only for the hardest rock climbing. I couldn't face retracing our steps down that waterfall and walking back across the desert. If we could only make the summit ... then we could cross the connecting ridge to the San Pedro Martir plateau and hike west through cool pines to the Meling Ranch. So we decided to go on; we were committed ... but to what? Uncertainty. We had no idea what obstacles lay ahead.

Earlier today Ogden told me a story:

A Zen man pursued by a tiger lowered himself over the edge of a cliff on a vine. Looking down he saw another tiger waiting below him. Looking up he saw that two mice had begun to gnaw through his vine. Directly in front of him a bunch of grapes were growing out of the cliff. Reaching out his hand he picked a grape and put it into his mouth. "Delicious!" he said.

Evening ... we were eating our grapes ... "our love," said Ogden. We bathed in the river and dried our bodies in the warm firelight. We drank a small bottle of red wine, ate Rye Crisp, finally slept on the windy ledge.

THURSDAY, FEBRUARY 9

And so next morning around one corner and behold—another waterfall. To bypass this one we struggled up a thirty-foot sheer drop, hauling ourselves on vines and tree branches. Above it the canyon widened and for a while we climbed on granite boulders until we were forced to drop into the riverbed and bushwhack again.

I will never forget this canyon. Its walls rise thousands of feet in tan gold granite. Its riverbed is dense with bushes and small trees, or choked with fallen slabs of stone. In the morning the light strikes the topmost crests of its walls hours before the shadows leave the canyon floor. At night the walls loom black against the stars.

We must have climbed a dozen waterfalls that day. We ate lunch in the sun above one of them—Rye Crisp, honey and an orange.

The water ran out. Still we found a few stagnant pools from which to fill our canteens. At dusk we camped in a sandy hollow beneath a huge boulder. Above us was the start of a great rock slide. Firelight's flickering shadows. Soup. Sleep.

FRIDAY, FEBRUARY 10

Slowly we begin to climb the rock slide. From here it is steep. The way is guarded by tall century plants. We circle around them, or thrust our way through their centers, repeatedly stabbed by their sharp swords. I am very tired. At noon the gorge opens into a hanging valley full of pine trees, sunlight and singing birds. We melt water from snow patches and cook underdone brown rice. I can't eat. I give my share to Ogden.

We have reached the head of the canyon. Our route is clear— up a long steep avalanche of boulders to where the canyon and the crest of a ridge meet in a sharp V on the skyline. Beyond there . . . we will not think further now.

I fall into my one-step-at-a-time mood and slowly my movement becomes a dance. Moving from boulder to boulder, I see every crack and tiny ledge in the rock. No motion is wasted. We stop to rest and the rhythm is broken; I never quite regain it.

Toward mid-afternoon we reach the bottom of the V. The boulders stop here and real rock climbing begins. We must climb up a polished slab of granite at a fifty-degree slope for maybe 600 feet, following the cracks water has worn in its surface. We take turns leading. It is scary. We are roped but have no pitons, no protection for the leader. We make it, pitch by pitch.

Dusk is coming, but Ogden wants to go one lead farther. By the time he is ready to belay me up it's almost dark and I can hardly see. I become terribly afraid, then angry, and am near furious tears when I reach the spot where he wants us to camp—a tiny ledge behind a pine tree, right on the face of the cliff.

It's too high, too exposed. I cling to Ogden and can't stop shaking. He builds a fire and we eat sardines, Rye Crisp, lemonade. Ogden is turned on by the danger of this hanging camp. I hate it. Finally I fix my bed on the hollowed-out ledge under the cliff, and squirm my way into my sleeping bag. Slowly I cheer up. It is really such a neat little hollow, perfectly fitting my body, that I regain my spirits. Ogden is on a steep angle, his feet braced against a rock. I am level and can sleep on my back or curl around a rock on my side. Mercifully, a large rock lies between me and the drop below. Strangely enough we both sleep deeply.

SATURDAY, FEBRUARY 11

We cross over the ridge at dawn, only to find lovely level places carpeted in pine needles not fifty yards from where we slept. We stop to make tea and eat a few raisins. Before us endless ridges rise to the south toward what may or may not be the summit.

I'm still very tired today. We climb slowly, stopping once to cook macaroni and cheese and melt snow for water. Near dusk we reach a crest and see what must be the summit far above us. We drop to camp in a windy notch between ridges. Soup . . . I eat some. Stars. Perhaps tomorrow. . . .

SUNDAY, FEBRUARY 12

I bathe with a little water, choke down a few mouthfuls of unsweetened oatmeal. The Instant Breakfast is strawberry, and I drink it. Solid food is tasteless and unpalatable. Liquids I can get down.

We climb on boulders through a forest of burned and leafless pines toward the ridge crest. Finally reach it and gaze out upon a fearful sight.

We are on the eastern rim of a steep canyon. Its walls are sheer. We cannot go around it on the knife-edged ridges. Somehow we must descend into the canyon and cross it if we are to go on . . . but how? Ogden's spirits drop to a frightening low. He has been watching the skyline and hoping for the summit for so long. "We'll find a way down," I say. Ogden doesn't answer. He just sits, staring in silence at the verticle drop below. I try to cheer him up with little success.

We build a fire on a bouldery ledge and cook instant mashed potatoes. Ogden eats them. I can't. Dubious ways out of our hanging position appear on either side. Finally I see a possible route, straight down the headwall from tree to tree as belay points. It goes. It takes us several hours, we have to rappel twice, but finally we find ourselves on the top of a traversable rock slide below the canyon face.

Ogden wants to continue the descent, down this side canyon to where it joins Diablo Canyon far below us, and from there climb out onto the plateau of the San Pedro Martir. I want to climb the opposite wall of the canyon face. I am convinced that from there we will see the summit. Ogden finally agrees.

It is vertical rock climbing. Plenty of holds, but we are very tired, so we rope up. Evening falls while we are still below the crest, and we are forced to camp on a small snow-covered ledge. Clouds are gathering in the west. We fix ourselves up as well as possible to weather a snowstorm, but both of us know we would probably be wiped out by one. We eat nothing. Somehow we sleep and the clouds blow over during the night.

I slipped and fell once that afternoon, unroped, when a rock broke off in my hand. Only a small pine tree kept me from plummeting 2,000 feet to my death, and I broke a finger, the small one on my left hand. I had no time to think anything—I only remember a wild scream as I fell.

MONDAY, FEBRUARY 13

We slowly reach the top of the face, climbing on icy rock with numb fingers, and see the summit, not far above us, and beyond it the ridge that leads out to the plateau. We are saved. I am exhausted.

In the sun below the summit we make tea, and, leaving our packs, we ascend to the north summit of El Picacho del Diablo. The south summit is too far away and too difficult for us to climb. We find the Summit Book in a heavy iron container and sign it, describing our route. We are glad to have made it, but not exhilarated or proud—we are too tired, almost out of food, and a long trial remains ahead of us—the tricky ridge to the plateau.

Climbing down from the summit takes all afternoon. We descend along a vertical crack where two walls meet at a ninety-degree angle, lowering our packs ahead of us with the rope. From there we cross several low ridges and climb to the beginning of the final ridge that connects El Picacho with the San Pedro Martir. A wind is rising. We camp on a small, semi-sheltered flat place in a notch. During the night a fierce windstorm begins, buffeting the trees above us with blasts of gale force. The storm keeps on through the morning and gray clouds blow in from the west. There is no question of going on.

THURSDAY, FEBRUARY 16
BELOW THE SUMMIT OF EL PICACHO

The storm lasted through Tuesday and Wednesday. We were sure that someone at home would miss us and send a search plane—we'd been gone two weeks instead of ten days—but no help came, and we lay in our bags, our spirits sinking lower and lower, and for the first time we considered the possibility that we might starve to death here.

We decided to try ESP, and I spent hours sending mental messages to Daddy: "I'm here, I'm on this mountain, help me," trying to make him hear.

I made Spanish rice and Ogden ate it. Finally today the storm ended and Ogden left.

It happened so fast. "I'll go for help," he said. "I'm still strong enough to hike, but if we wait maybe I won't be. You stay here."

"OK," I said. Too tired to think of hiking. Too tired to think at all.

He packed his gear—sleeping bag, one package of instant mashed potatoes, Ensolite pad—walked twenty feet to the edge of this level spot, turned smiling with his arm raised in a victory sign, and then he was gone.

Now I am alone.

5

The Witches' Dance

From the Journal of Francis Dart, 1967

THURSDAY, FEBRUARY 16, 1967
EUGENE, OREGON

I was so tired today after the last few days of lectures and meetings that I went to bed early while Alice was out to a Friends Meeting committee session. About nine o'clock Marjorie Kellogg, Ogden's mother, called up from Gold Hill to say that Ogden and Eleanor had not yet returned from Mexico. They should have got back to Claremont three days ago, and Ogden's roommate, Gordon Bailey, is worried and had called her. They are trying to learn more and will call again tomorrow. Ogden, Sr., may fly down there tomorrow.

We have been waiting to hear from Eleanor. Now I too am worried.

FRIDAY, FEBRUARY 17

I talked with my brother Leonard by phone this morning. He says there is considerable alarm that Ogden and Eleanor have not been heard from. They had intended to go to San Felipe on the east side of Baja California, cross over the San Pedro de Martir mountains, probably climbing El Picacho del Diablo, the highest one, and then go on to a ranch on the west side. A number of people say that it is a long way across and they may simply have underestimated the time needed.

Gordon Bailey will drive down toward the Rancho San Jose today or tomorrow to look for them.

This evening both Leonard and Marjorie called. There is still no word from Ogden or Eleanor. Ogden, Sr., flew to San Diego today—his parents live in La Jolla. He and Gordon Bailey are driving down the west side of the San Pedro Mountains, and he expects to rent a plane to fly over the area. There are few roads and very poor communications. The Mexican "Green Patrol" (highway patrol?) have been alerted, and the American consul is making inquiries on the east side as well.

It is said that there are ranches, cowboys, etc., scattered widely on the west side of the mountain range and that water is available there. It would be possible for hikers who are lost or sick to be taken in and cared for for some time without word getting out to where there are roads or telephones. Ogden does speak Spanish and he has been to this area before. In a way this offers some encouragement, but I am greatly worried just the same, and I know Alice is even more so.

Leonard and Marjorie both say there is nothing I can do down there. I do so wish Eleanor had left better information about their plans. It is not in her nature (nor in his, I guess) just now to do so—she thinks "independence" is to have no one know where you are or what you are doing. She even checked out of her dorm before leaving, so was not missed right away.

SATURDAY, FEBRUARY 18

It has been a long, long day, and still no real information. Leonard says that there is practically no communication in most of the area involved. Statements, or rumors, indicate Eleanor and

24

Ogden did get to San Felipe, but little more, except that apparently they did not yet reach the Meling ranch.

I have tried to say, through Leonard, that the danger is at the mountain. Of course they may have been delayed hiking out or they may be at some ranch, but if so they are all right, however much we worry. But I feel sure that the mountain itself must be the place to search. If it were not a difficult climb Eleanor would not have traveled that far to climb it. Gordon Bailey says that they were not going to climb it all the way if it proved difficult, and were not going to climb the east face in any case, but *if* they are in trouble on the mountain itself, then they need help *soon*.

Now another night lies ahead. I dread the nights. In the day I am aware of my fears, but I can concentrate on work and succeed part of the time in passing the time just by working. The night is like a long drawn-out fantasy, a kind of witches' dance.

You are so tired that surely you must sleep this time. Then you begin to ask, "Is there something more I could tell them that might help?"

Then slowly, so slowly, you see them on the mountain where they have slipped and are trapped on a ledge. Waiting for you. Then they are dead beside a road where they were attacked and robbed. You see each detail and as you finally convince yourself that this is not reasonable, that the Mexican farmers are friendly people, the picture dissolves. But you see them again, on the desert this time. They left the mountain but got lost in the desert. There is no water and they are barely alive. Come quickly! Soon it is the mountain again. They fell and you see them broken and crumpled beneath a cliff. There is no help for them, but at least their bodies might be found.

This goes on all night, grotesque in its slowness, gruesome in its vivid images. Who can go to sleep when Eleanor is right there injured and calling, "Daddy, I need you. Help me, help me."

Someone suggested that they have merely gone off to get married. Maybe they will turn up in a few days in Canada, happy and unconcerned. But I know better.

Alice will take a sleeping tablet tonight. She needs it. I'll not. I think one of us should be ready to answer the phone.

◆

Journal of Eleanor Dart
THURSDAY, FEBRUARY 16
BELOW THE SUMMMIT OF EL PICACHO

Ogden's is the struggle now. He will hike down into Diablo Canyon 2,000 feet below, and from there climb the ridge of the San Pedro Martir onto the hilly plateau we have been gazing at for a week across the deep canyon. He'll try to find the Rancho San Jose, using a compass and a sketchy map of Baja. If he succeeds, a plane should come to rescue me. If not, I may starve to death here.

I couldn't go with him. I am too weak, not having eaten more than a few mouthfuls of rice in five days. So he finally has his chance to be a hero. And my task is to wait and survive as long as I can.

After he left I fixed up my camp and set out the rescue blanket my brother Paul gave me for Christmas, weighting it down with stones. It flashes metallic gold in the sunlight—perhaps some passing plane will see it. Then I fetched snow to melt for water and collected enough firewood for tonight. While doing so I found this nook I am sitting in. But the wind is rising again and I will have to crawl back into my sleeping bag.

It's a beautiful place to wait as long as the wind stays down. High on a ridge of El Picacho del Diablo, walled in on either side by giant granite gendarmes, I must be at least at 9,000 feet. To the southeast lie descending rocky ridges of the mountain. Beyond them a flat desert basin edged by low hills, and beyond the hills a blue strip that is the Sea of Cortez. To the north is the long ridge of the San Pedro Martir. I look across Diablo Canyon to the crest of the ridge and I can see the sloping forested plateau that hides the Rancho San Jose—the promised land.

I am sitting in a small hollow carpeted with pine needles, leaning on a boulder. Directly in front of me is a wind-twisted cypress, like a Japanese painting against the sky. Its upper branches are bare and gray, weathered in lines like the pattern of skin cells on a dirty hand. They stand out against the moving clouds.

Writing helps me forget the emptiness in my stomach.

FRIDAY, FEBRUARY 17

Two chickadees just visited my pine tree, hopping from branch to branch in their black caps and neckbands and white waistcoats, chirping loudly. It is my sixth day without food. I am sitting in the same place, stark naked except for my hat. The sun is very hot and there is no real wind. I smell strong—like a human cow barn.

Last night I read "Out of the Cradle Endlessly Rocking" by Walt Whitman. I watched the sun set and built a fire to make tea. There was bright moonlight and no wind. As I lay down to sleep I no longer felt any anxiety. I felt at one with nature, at home and protected. The mountains, the wind, my body—all were a unity and there was nothing to fear. I was glad Ogden left. Better he should go, even though it meant leaving me here alone, than wait together to starve to death. I have never been all alone in the wilderness for so long before. I decided to enjoy it.

I couldn't sleep. I was excruciatingly uncomfortable, tangled in clothes, damp between the legs, on an incline I kept sliding down. I tossed and turned and planned feverishly, thinking about Ogden, planning our house and our future. Finally toward dawn

I slept fitfully, then climbed up here to watch the sunrise. Red clouds above the Sea of Cortez gained in brilliance, pulsing with light until the sun rose out of their white hot center.

I sat for two hours as the sun slowly gained altitude, then slept.

I am very weak. I sway when I walk and have to rest, panting, after any exertion.

Why doesn't someone back home send a search party to look for us? We are almost a week overdue now.

In the afternoon I carved a tiny pine wood totem for Ogden in the shape of a man. Then I mended my pants—or tried to. They were terribly ripped. I built a fire before dark and made tea, then lay down in my sleeping bag at sunset under a bright half-moon.

SATURDAY, FEBRUARY 18

The mornings are beautiful. All the earth lies around me and at my feet. I saw a tiny furry chipmunk, dark brown. I think he stole the lid from my tea box. There is a robber jay who caws loudly and occasionally dive bombs just above my head with a metallic WHIRRRRR! in passing. I heard a new bird voice for a while today—one short call like a prolonged musical hiccup, repeated at intervals. A flock of tiny black and white birds stopped in my cypress, chattering musically. I am a Zen hermit fasting in the mountains.

I read Walt Whitman's "Specimen Days," about his hospital work during the Civil War. It occurs to me that this mountain time alone is a good thing. I can use it to slow down and look at my life. I think about school and Ogden and our plans for marrying next summer. I see that I will be able to continue studying and that our life will be good. I plan our wedding, our farm, the garden I'll plant.

The afternoons are not so good. I hear several high-flying planes, but none see me here. I realize how weak I am becoming. My hands shake when I try to whittle, my heart beats fast and my breath comes in gasps when I walk fifty feet to get snow. My legs are wobbly and my balance uncertain. I must go very slowly downhill. I am dizzy.

I must fetch snow for water and gather firewood. The trips are painful, yet I must make them. I have visions of myself several days from now crawling across these rocks to get water.

How long? I know Ogden can't have reached any habitation yet—it's too far, he's only been gone two days—and still I listen for the plane that never comes. Where is he?

He could be lost, hurt, dead. Perhaps no plane will ever come and I'll just grow weaker and weaker. All these plans that I am making—are they only dreams? If I am to die here ... it is a beautiful place to die, but I don't want to die. My plans are beautiful too.

I am hungry in the afternoons. My stomach growls. Occasionally I allow myself to think about a ham sandwich on white bread with lettuce and a giant juicy dill pickle. Or pancakes, light and golden brown, covered with apricot-pineapple jam. But mostly I avoid thoughts of food. The tea brew is good and cool.

My bladder has begun to leak urine continuously. I am always damp.

So I busy myself with reading, mending, whittling, sunbathing, writing. I comb my hair. I fetch snow. I sit in the sun thinking nothing, grateful just to be at rest. And through it all I dread the night.

The night ... with brilliant moonlight and stars (Orion's right shoulder is red). The night ... freezing cold and sleepless.

I have developed insomnia. I toss and turn on the hard ground, cramped, bound by clothing, always uncomfortable. My mind is fantastically busy ... planning, dreaming, scheming. I get frantic claustrophobia inside my down bag. I long to jump off a cliff just to end this exhausted activity, but I am too tired to stand up. My feet are icy cold. Finally toward morning I fall into interrupted dozing.

I dread the night. How many more nights? I can bear the days, but the nights will drive me insane.

In the mornings I believe I could still hike out of here if no help comes. In the afternoons I know I could never do that, not even 200 yards, and I listen for a plane. At night I plan for the future and know my plans may never come true, and dream of death with a heavy heart.

I can accept death in the mornings, but at night it frightens me, and I long for the end of this waiting.

SATURDAY, FEBRUARY 18, EVENING

It's getting cold and a wind is rising. Night is coming again. Oh my God . . . how long?

I started to make up my bed and get firewood for the night. . . . Oh joy . . . tremulous, fearful, wonderful hope. A small plane just flew out of the west. I waved my red sweater. As it approached the mountain it came quite low, banked steeply and circled the peak, flew by above me to the south and then off again into the west. I waved the whole time. They *must* have seen me.

Perhaps Ogden reached the Rancho San Jose—they have an air field—and the plane came out signaling to me that someone knows I am here and help is coming. It *must* be so.

I am trembling all over. I did not realize I had lost so much hope. I am almost crying.

Please let it be so. Soon, perhaps tomorrow, surely tomorrow. I can bear the night now with this hope to hold on to. Thank you for this sign, Ogden, Providence, God. I am so shaken that I'm almost sick.

I must find firewood now—it's getting colder and the night is close.

It's amazing the difference the sight of that one small plane has made to my spirits. I hope I wasn't hallucinating. It came and went so quickly. I think . . . if Ogden made it to the ranch and sent the plane, then he's warm and clean and well fed by now. It makes it so much easier to be cold and hungry, just believing that.

6

Empty Skies

From the Journal of Francis Dart

SUNDAY, FEBRUARY 19
EUGENE, OREGON

Leonard called to say nothing has been found. There are various rumors. The search is increasing, so the consul says. Police are contacting all the ranches in the whole area. No smoke or signal has been seen from the mountain. He does not know whether a real ground search of the mountain has been started. I *know* this must be done. Leonard will urge the consul, who does not seem anxious to do this. Planes from the San Diego Sheriff's Patrol have flown over the mountain and western plateau without finding anything. Helicopters might be obtained from San Diego but have not yet been brought in.

People in Meeting [Quaker Meeting for Worship] are so helpful. They are worried too, but they do want to help. It is also a help to be together with Alice and Paul all day. I know that Paul feels the worry, but he is careful not to increase it, to talk of other things and to be cheerful. We all are "cheerful." What good is that, when there is such a weight that I can't seem to bear it?

Marjorie Kellogg called. Her husband feels very encouraged,

she says. The country to the west is really not bad. Then why are they still missing? Poor Marjorie is alone and completely helpless to do anything. I have never seen her, but I know her voice now, and something of her spirit.

Another night beginning.

MONDAY, FEBRUARY 20

I am so tired. I can meet my classes, but it is hard to work alone. Soon the witches will dance day and night.

If Eleanor is dead, what then? She went on her own decision, at her own wish. She is old enough to decide things for herself. People do die. Is it necessarily so bad?

I think death is not really so bad itself. But what if she is not dead but only caught somewhere, needing help. What if she went there only to get away from me? For all these past weeks she has been so mixed up and troubled in spirit. I have tried to help; I have really tried, but I have not helped. In any case it is not right for her to die. She is only just ready to begin life. She holds so very much promise. It can't all go to nothing now.

Sometimes these last days it seems strange to me that it should matter so much to us now when, in a sense, we are about to lose her anyway. Within just a few years, even now almost, we'll only see her once in a while, and we'll have no responsibility for her at all. But it does matter. It does.

Leonard called up again. No news.

TUESDAY, FEBRUARY 21

Alice called me up just after lunch. They are found! They are all right! They walked out to a place called Valle Trinidad and are on the way to San Felipe. The newspaper telephoned the news to her.

I feel light-headed and unsteady—as one does when one takes off a heavy pack—except that it is inside. I meet my honors class and tell them all about it, although I had not mentioned anything about it before. I tell people in the hall or people I know. I go home to rejoice with Alice. She has sent a message to Paul in school. We can rest.

This evening it was in the newspaper with Eleanor's picture. Then a radio report said that this news *was not confirmed*, that the consul in Mexicali was continuing the search! A horrible premonition came over me as I knew the report was not true. I went out to a lecture filled with foreboding.

I got back to find Alice had just finished talking with Leonard. The report of their being found is not true. He thinks I should go down there. I called him to say I'll be in Pomona about 10:30 tomorrow morning, then packed up a sleeping bag, etc. Paul gave me his compass and match holder.

I will try to sleep.

WEDNESDAY, FEBRUARY 22
SAN FELIPE, BAJA

We were up about 5:00 A.M. in plenty of time for the early plane to Portland. From there direct to L.A. past all the Cascade peaks she has climbed so much. Mother and Gordon Bailey met me at Pomona.

At Leonard's everything is in a sort of orderly confusion. Telephone messages, notes, people offering help, people asking for news. Ann Urey came with packs and camp food. Pomona College Zoology Department will lend their Land Rover. Steven Schaffran will come with us. He speaks good Spanish—two years Peace Corps in Peru. Several people offer to fly their planes when needed.

We left about mid-afternoon, drove over to Palm Springs, Indio and past the Salton Sea to El Centro and Calexico. Supper. Called the consulate. Mr. Feldman, the consul, and Ogden, Sr., are in San Felipe where we are to meet them. We crossed into Mexicali, bought insurance for the Landrover and headed south. The road is straight and good. I could not see much by moonlight except that the country is flat and seems dry. There are hills to the west.

By eleven we saw lights out to sea, maybe fishing boats, then we were in San Felipe and soon met Feldman and Ogden, Sr., at the Motel Cortez. They told us of more rumors and of plans for tomorrow. The rumors are not convincing and offer no hope.

Eleanor and Ogden definitely were here and left on February 5th or 6th. They were given a ride inland toward Trinidad from a point twenty miles north of here by a white pickup truck with several people in it. Tomorrow we start at 4:30 A.M. to join several police units in a sweep of that valley to find this truck and its owner.

This sounds well organized, but I am appalled. The consul and police are treating the whole thing as though it is either a case of crime or of runaways. The crime angle is their business to check, but it seems very unlikely. The runaway bit is simply not believable.

They have not even started to search the mountain.

It is cold here at night. The motel faces right out on the gulf. While the consul and police chief go out to chase down a rumor that Ogden just came into San Felipe on the night bus, we will try to rest. They may find someone, but it won't be Ogden.

◆

Journal of Eleanor Dart
SUNDAY MORNING, FEBRUARY 19
EL PICACHO DEL DIABLO

Another storm is rising today—the wind is freezing cold and no help has come. I am leaning against a tree completely bundled in tarp, sleeping bag, clothes and gloves. It is about 10:00 A.M.

Still no sign of a plane. If no one comes today I will despair. I have a really bad sore throat—must be catching a cold.

Oh little plane, what did you mean? Someone must come . . . someone . . .

LATER

My spirits have risen a little. I moved camp up to a sunny spot above the cypress and set up a windbreak with my poncho and some twine. To do so took all my energy. I often began to faint and had to sit down suddenly. After a while I will bring the rest of my gear up here. I think this must be my last move. I haven't strength enough to move again. How I will get water from here I'm not sure; it is a long way to the snow. And there is no place for a fire. But I am more sheltered.

Still no one has come. It is almost noon. Little plane, were you sent only to mock me, or were you a dream?

I feel quite sick to my stomach (what there is left of it) today. I don't see how anyone *could* rescue me in this wind even if they were to try.

I combed my hair and put on lipstick and that raised my spirits some. I really am very dizzy and faint and nauseated. I wonder how long I will be able to move about at all. A few days I imagine, if I go very slowly.

I am not resigned to death.

How can I bear to leave this world? How can I give it all up? My mother, my father, sister, brother . . . the wild western ocean . . . all the lands and rooms and flowers and rivers that I have never touched.

To breathe the air. To be healthy, running in autumn leaves and wind. Just life, just life . . . what is it that I value so? What is it I cannot bear to leave?

And so the wind blows and the sky stretches above me, and I know that all my outraged crying makes no difference. If I die, I die, and I have no control over the matter. But I cannot accept it. I pray, plead, make bargains, yearn, wish, protest. Will I ever accept it? Or will I die protesting passionately. . . .

Evening is coming again. No sign of help. I am losing my faith in rescuers. I suspect that if a helicopter does come I will look up without putting down my book and observe dispassionately, "The helicopter is a mythical beast," then resume my reading.

MONDAY, FEBRUARY 20

A routine has emerged—wake as sun hits me. When it warms up, sit against tree by bed until the sun is high, writing. Move to upper spot and set up windbreak. Exhausted from this effort, nap. Sunbathe until shadows come. Read Whitman or whittle. Before dusk set up bed, make fire if not windy; if windy, go to bed.

Spent today in great anguish of spirit. No help came. Death, I am afraid of you. Wind rose at evening.

TUESDAY, FEBRUARY 21

BEATITUDE

After a night of freezing storm winds
Silent air of morning,
Sunlight's warm blessing on my cheek,
Cloudless sky.
A drink of cool water.
Chickadee twittering in pines.

The night was below freezing, gale-strength winds buffeting me all night. A continuous struggle to keep my feet warm. I am very tired and sick this morning.

I woke to a realization: if Ogden is alive, then help is surely coming and it doesn't matter how soon. I must stay alive until it comes.

If Ogden is not alive, then death will not be so hard to take. My future is so tied to him that without him it seems hollow. I still don't want death, but it is easier to accept that way.

I think I can be patient now; I feel at rest in the quiet after the storm. It still is not easy physically—I am shaky and nauseated, and will be sicker. I'm always cold. But spiritually I am finding some inner peace at last.

WEDNESDAY, FEBRUARY 22

I am setting out to try climbing the ridge to the San Pedro Martir. I'm afraid Ogden has been killed and I've got to save my own life. I just climbed out and scouted the route he took down the mountain. I could see it leads down to a vertical drop. I don't think he made it.

I can't wait to starve any longer. I'll just go a little ways each day. I may have to turn back or get stuck, but I'll try to stay in the open, in sight of planes.

A desperate move—I haven't eaten in ten days now. I've got to die trying. I'll make it. I have to.

7

"Mucho bello—Mucho malo"

From the Journal of Francis Dart

We were up to an early breakfast of eggs, coffee and bread as the San Felipe portion of a posse got together. Other contingents will meet us from Mexicali and Ensenada. By the time the forces had met at the turn-off from the highway the search for the pickup truck was unnecessary. Its driver had heard about the missing couple and volunteered to show us where he let them off. This took courage, and he is obviously frightened, but I think truthful too.

He showed us where he let them off thirty miles or so from the highway at the northwest corner of a long flat desert valley. He says it was about ten or eleven at night and very windy and cold. They wanted to get out sooner, but he thought better to let them off near some shelter—here in the pass there is a stone police hut. It appears to be a long way to the mountain across barren desert.

We talked with the driver. Steve Shaffran is at ease with the language both linguistically and culturally. Leonard and the San Felipe police chief went off to hire some Indians to help search. Then we all moved down the valley to the Santa Clara ranch,

39

sending parties to other ranches to inquire. The track is very sandy and often deep in dust. There is a large dry lake bed, but the rest of it is through cactus and thorn tree desert. We have a Green Patrol radio truck, a fire department rescue wagon, a couple of jeeps and the Land Rover.

The whole operation has a certain play-acting character about it, at least it seemed so to me. I can help drive, but I cannot do much else, and I see no real hope in what is being done. However, one thing I can do, and I know how to do it if I just don't lose patience. If only I am in time.

By mid-afternoon, with invaluable help from Steve, I had established that there are no Mexicans, official or otherwise, around here who have ever climbed this mountain or even know much about it. I think I have convinced Mr. Feldman (at what cost in doubts of my own) that Eleanor and Ogden have *not* simply gone off on a lark to Mexico City. If they are on the mountain then they can't get off by themselves and they can't signal. Then it is desperately urgent that we search the mountain *with real mountaineers*. The Mexicans here cannot do this and will not object to Americans doing it.

Then came a break that may be important. We reached the last ranch southward to find that tracks had been observed in Providencia Canyon, tracks representing two people—one large, one smaller. It is a frightful looking canyon.

By evening Ogden, Sr., and Mr. Feldman had started for Mexicali to get some mountaineers from the Sierra Club. Steve had gone with them to return to school. Leonard and I took Gill (the police chief) back to San Felipe. We'll return tomorrow.

FRIDAY, FEBRUARY 24
DESERT EAST OF EL PICACHO

We got up to a clear sky with a strong breeze blowing in from the Gulf and had breakfast, joined by Gill. Then we went over to the tourist bureau office where we were to receive a radio message from Mr. Feldman concerning American mountaineers. I stayed there to wait while Leonard and Gill rounded up gas and food. The office (which opens at 8:30) did open shortly before 10:00 but could get no radio contact with Mexicali. About 10:30 we took Gill to the airport, where he got a ride out to the dry lake with an American tourist who has a plane here.

Leonard and I then drove out the "Santa Clara Freeway"— about thirty miles of rough sand and rock road across the desert—with a Mexican boy as a guide. We got out to the ranch about noon. A party had gone to look for tracks at Diablo Canyon; a plane from San Diego had come and gone again. No news. No news is bad news.

This afternoon, with nothing else to do, I had plenty of time to look at the east face of the mountain. It is big. A massive pyramid of granite cliffs and crevasses, entered along its base by a number of steep rocky canyons that start with talus fans on the desert floor and quickly develop into narrow steep-sided slashes that end finally in the face itself. It is scarred by many cracks and chimneys and buttressed with imposing vertical-sided gendarmes. One can imagine possible routes to the summit. None look easy.

There is vegetation here and there at higher elevations and there are patches of snow. Water. I scan the cliffs with my glasses looking for a sign—smoke, a colored blanket or jacket. Nothing. I recall Steve's cheerful word to the rancher when the mountain was glowing in the early sunset: "*Mucho bello*," and the other's impassive reply: "*Mucho malo*."

Late in the afternoon two cars arrived with members of the San Diego Sierra Club. Ropes, packs, camp gear, food. After some conferring they decided to camp at the mouth of Providencia Canyon tonight and search it tomorrow. I will join them while Leonard drives Gill back to San Felipe.

I have unrolled my bed under a clear sky near the canyon mouth. We have a good, but dry, camp. We no sooner arrived than the leader of this group, "Bud" Bernhard, started up the canyon alone to look for tracks. He got back out after dark to report that there are clear tracks heading up the canyon and back out. He is sure that the tracks coming out are several days more recent than those going in and are only a few days old. He feels sure these are their tracks, and he is convinced that they are not in this canyon now.

This is very puzzling to me, for this is almost the southernmost canyon, and they approached from the north. Why did they come here, and if they came out again, where did they go then? Mr. Bernhard knows this mountain. I do not, but I know Eleanor, and so we must put our knowledge together. He is impulsive, busy and in a hurry, and somewhat officious. Not easy to talk to. But he is obviously sincerely determined to help and he seems to know his business.

The others are younger, strong and enthusiastic, but not familiar with this area. They were driven down here by two older club members who are also camping here, as are the two Indian trackers Leonard hired. There have been several car lights visible across the valley at the ranch or dry lake. More people coming? A message? There is no knowing tonight.

I am glad to be out here under this mountain tonight. I wish Eleanor could know that we are here, that we are really trying, that at last we are coming up on the mountain where I am sure she is.

I am tired and very much depressed. As the night grows colder I can feel her calling. I am so afraid we are too late.

SATURDAY, FEBRUARY 25

We were up at daylight, a somewhat cloudy morning, and after some breakfast, we could talk a little. Then Bernhard took three men with him to search Diablo Canyon for tracks, leaving me and one of the others to keep camp, and the two Indians to look for tracks leaving the canyon mouth. After a couple of hours we heard someone approaching up the road and went out to meet a group of three or four members of the Sierra Madre Mountain Rescue Group. They had complete equipment including two-way radio sets with them, said they had set up a base camp on the lake bed and were on their way up Providencia Canyon. Then they listened to what we had to say, reported it in to their base and directed me there.

I got to the lake bed to find a bustle of well-organized activity. Several vehicles were there, a camp was being created, a landing strip had been marked out and there were two planes in already. The leader of this operation, Ray, was dividing his men into groups and dispatching one group into each probable canyon, and another to start up where Eleanor and Ogden got out of the truck, prepared to track them wherever they went. Communication was arranged between each group and the base camp by radio, relayed where necessary from a plane. The search has suddenly been transformed into a large-scale, highly systematic operation.

I feel much more encouraged and even cheerful enough to watch the operation with admiration and to notice with interest a subtle change in attitude that began as I talked with Ray and others about Eleanor and Ogden. They already know all about their equipment—they had mimeographed data with them giving probable clothing, types of shoes, size and tread, packs, food, etc. Where did they get all this? But they know hardly anything about the actual people they are searching for.

I spoke about Eleanor. She has taken at least two climbing schools, has climbed most of the Cascade peaks, is experienced, careful, more likely to be slow than impetuous. She is physically strong with lots of stamina. She is level-headed in a crisis. As I told Ray these things some of the grimness in his appearance was replaced by relief and even a bit later by cheerful determination.

Of course there is another thing. I know there have been suggestions (and rumors to support them) that Eleanor and Ogden are not on the mountain nor west of it. That they have gone off to Mexico City or maybe Canada and that we will hear from them in due time via a cheerful phone call. What can I say if this even might be true. These men are not just giving up a couple of day's wages and the cost of driving to Mexico—they are risking their own safety on a dangerous mountain, preparing to search the worst places as well as the best, flying airplanes into these narrow canyons with their turbulent winds. It is a matter of faith and of confidence in Eleanor, even though I scarcely know Ogden at all.

I cannot present an argument. I can only say that I *know* she would go off only after telling us, if at all. That I *know* she is somewhere where she cannot get word to anyone. That she may be in trouble on the mountain or may be dead on the mountain.

By evening we are no longer looking for two young students who may have run off together. We are mountaineers searching for fellow mountaineers.

The day has produced a lot of information. The tracking group found their tracks starting across the desert and found their camp. Tracks have been found going in and out of Diablo Canyon above the falls, but not very far up. The tracks in Providencia go a long way up. There are tracks and a camp in Diablito Canyon. Here the tracks go up only, none came out. This is disheartening, for Diablito is a "mistake route" taken sometimes by people who mistake it for Diablo Canyon. It leads to a nearly impossible face. I found a small tag at the entrance to Diablito reading, "Road's end Diablito Canyon. Diablo Falls two miles." One could misunderstand this and be led by it up Diablito. Are they up there somewhere?

At a conference this afternoon Bernhard pointed out that it is possible to cross a ridge from Diablito and descend into Diablo Canyon or even to drop into Providencia Canyon. Hence the in-and-out tracks in these may not be what they seem. We must search much farther up each of these, which will take more time. We really need to know whether they ever got to the summit.

It was decided to try for a helicopter in order to check the register at the summit and Ogden, Sr., who had rented a jeep and driven back down here, flew up to Mexicali in Norman Illsley's plane to try to get one.

Since this seems very doubtful it was decided to send a ground party up to the summit too, starting at dawn tomorrow. It is a two-day trip each way, and there will be difficulty finding people who can give the time to go. Bernhard will go and wants to start tonight. Several others say they cannot. An older man from the Montrose Sierra Club, here with his wife, said quietly, "I'm a mountaineer, and if I am hung up on a mountain sometime I want someone to come looking for me. That is why I'm here now and I'll go up. I'll stay here a month if necessary."

The pilots report a storm front coming in north of San Diego and it has been clouding up all afternoon. Before sunset we could see that it was raining or snowing up on the mountain, and there is a strong wind blowing down here on the lake bed.

Steve Schaffran came back with Norman. He is camping with Leonard and me out on the salt flat. I want to sleep and I cannot. There is so much in my mind. Admiration for these people around me, pilots and climbers who are also brick masons, telephone employees, electronic engineers, artists. Hope—sometimes as their tracks or a camp has been found and reported, they seem so near. Fear—having come so close, will we be defeated now by weather.

Behind it all a terrible blank is growing. We are too late. It has been too long and we will not find them alive. We may not find them at all.

I fight it back and sometimes I win for a while. But the blank cloud is always there, ready to win in its time.

◆

Journal of Eleanor Dart
THURSDAY MORNING, FEBRUARY 23
EL PICACHO DEL DIABLO

Got to top of the next gendarme yesterday. Camped in sort of cave. *Gorgeous* sunset. Prayed for Ogden. God let him be alive. Can move better in afternoons. Freezing cold. One more gendarme to go—a bad one.

4:00 P.M. Friends, I've had it. I made it down the gendarme I was on. Many rappels. Took me darn near four to five hours. I had a good long look at the climb across to the San Pedro Martir and it just won't go, I daren't try it. Besides which I am too damn weak to go uphill hardly at all.

So tomorrow I start suicide route number two, which I maybe should have done to begin with. Down Diablo Canyon and across the desert to the La Trinidad road. I'm scared, frankly. They say there is one helluva big waterfall in there somewhere. And no rescue plane is going to be able to see me in that canyon. I'm on my own with a vengeance. The desert scares me too—twenty miles of it. No other choice though. Now I'll try to patch my pants.

FRIDAY, FEBRUARY 24

Warm camp Thursday night behind fallen log.

Planes. Didn't see me—buzzing the canyon. Long hard day down to rockslide between gendarmes and halfway down to camp beneath rock. *Uncomfortable*. Rained. Up early so can get down into Arroyo del Diablo.

SATURDAY, FEBRUARY 25

Down into river valley at last. Water cheering. Saw Cedar Camp and Sierra Club markers.

Damn. I've really botched it this time. Yesterday a little plane started a diligent search for me, looking in all the low places. I was too high for them to see, going down. Today I finally made it down into the canyon and now they are searching all the high places. I wave, but they never see me. It is so frustrating.

I really haven't the strength to go on any farther. I was a fool to think I could get myself out of here. So I've parked in the most open place I can find, set out as many markers as I can muster, and as Martin Luther said, "Here I stand. I can do no other."

Surely they'll see me eventually? I've been so stupid this trip. I never should have left the ridge at all. I should have known Ogden would be OK.

Please, little plane, come down to my level. It could be a long wait.

I dreamed last night about an enormous dinner, milkshakes for dessert. Last night was one of the most excruciating I have ever had. On rocky sand, hard as cement, and it rained.

Later: all day plane overhead, never sees me. Despair. I climb hill, hear a voice calling, "Help. . . ." Is it Ogden? The route he planned to go down is frightful to see—huge rockpiles dropping off into vertical cliffs.

8

Devil Mountain

From the Journal of Eleanor Dart

I swear to God I am damn frustrated. Two helicopters overhead all morning. Close overhead. I flash at them with top of first-aid kit, wave a sweater. Do they see me? No. They never look *down*. So finally I build a smoky fire—dirty brown smoke and they don't see *that*. They're just *set* on looking high. I swear I'm beat. I don't know what more I can do. I can *hear* 'em up there, buzzing around out of sight, but they just won't see me. Maybe they're playing army games and aren't really looking for me at all.

I guess actually my smoke all gets blown up the canyon and ain't visible enough to see. Well, I can't even hear them anymore. "Hell, baby," as my black friend Lincoln says, maybe I'll die here yet. Or maybe they found Ogden, maybe that's it.

One thing I'll grant. They are being most thorough about searching the upper slopes of the mountain. If and when they ever decide to search the canyon (pray God they will) they can't help but find me. There's hope at least.

I N

ease let them find him. Of course, as I
doing the right thing. If we are on the
h worse trouble than if we are in the
first place to search. But I'm assailed
aid they'll *never* search this canyon and
They *must* search here eventually, but

y anyway.
hadows in the valley, and cold. It is nice
ith, they'll find me someday. If not . . .
Daddy took us all out for a Chinese
in, ginger beef, bean sprouts, crisp bean
sweet and sour pork, won ton mein . . .
strawberry waffles. I haven't been hun-
much about food, I mean—until now.
must be going crazy with worry. Until
hed with my own survival to give them
There's nothing I can do. And Ogden's
t was his voice I heard, let them find
him soon.

Let's talk about religion and faith for a bit. Mine has gone up
and down this trip. Last night, believing that the search was over
and I would die here, I felt very full of faith. Funny, at my lowest
points I seem to find strength in some power, some Dharma, a
sure way of things. Once I have to let go of fighting for my life
with my own powers, I find peace and inner strength.

I've read the proofs of God's existence and the proofs of the
opposite, and I'm sure that there *is* no proof, just this inner peace
that comes when "all our strivings cease." That Quaker hymn
means a lot to me just now—let go, let go of desires and passions
and being fixed on some concrete goal, and let the "still dew of
quietness" descend. Find the "beauty of thy peace" even in death.
Especially in death, for what else have we to cling to then?

I don't find inner peace too often. I'm too obsessed with striv-
ing. But it is there.

And I've never been sure about praying. I've always felt I mustn't pray for help until I was absolutely unable to do anything myself, and then perhaps it was only a desperate appeal to a nonexistent power. But prayer needn't be an appeal; it may be a simple letting go, essentially saying, "It is in your hands now, as it always was, although I was too blind to see it."

I've thought a lot about death this trip, and mostly I've been afraid when I felt I was really up against it. A terrible fear, followed by a grim resolution that by God I would *not* sit and wait helplessly to die. I'd get out of this if I had to *crawl* twenty miles across that desert. I'd fight until I couldn't move a muscle—and then? Ah . . . what then?

Mostly I've refused to think "and then." But I've begun to realize that I can't make it out of here myself—*probably . . . I won't admit it yet*—and sometimes I've thought "and then." When I do I begin to find that peace again, and I believe I will find it more strongly as I grow weaker.

I look around and feel this wouldn't be so bad a place to weaken and die. I am sitting on warm sand above the creek, leaning on a boulder. The granite around me sparkles in the sun. Below me I hear the water gurgling and rushing . . . ah, sweet water . . . I've lived on water for days and days now.

The helicopters are gone . . . instead there is a silver plane. . . . How to conquer fear? Let go, let go, accept death, wait.

Often now I hear singing voices in the water, barely audible, like a trio of women's voices, soft and susurrant, now faint, now rushing . . . making pleasant harmony just because it is their nature to do so and the day is so beautiful.

The leafy bushes and trees near my creek are full of birds—gray, black and white robber jays, chickadees, tiny yellow and brown sparrows that chirp and twitter. I could never catch and eat one. I should try, but they are so pretty.

And insects—water skaters on the pools and little white moth-like creatures that light on my hands. Flies, inevitably, and honey hornets—they take honey from the pea green shoots of the young willow buds. I tried them today while on a "survival hike" and they aren't bad, but *so* tiny.

I might be able to live on algae. The stream is full of slimy pea green strands of it. Perhaps I'll try it tomorrow.

I saw a young spruce in the woods yesterday—startlingly fresh and green, and it gladdened my heart.

I'm happy when it's sunny. My spirits seem to fluctuate with the weather and rise and fall with the sun. But the stars are beautiful too. Orion, old friend, was there last night, and the full moon.

I hate the cold, though. I wish I could keep the fire going all night. There's plenty of wood, though it takes so much energy to get it. Perhaps I can bank the fire, but I doubt it, and when my matches run out I'll be unhappy.

And then there is the mountain—awesome, rocky, terrible above me, casting me in shadow. I fear this mountain now. I know how deadly it can be. I know how the wind blows freezing cold up there. Yes, we climbed it, a real accomplishment . . . and to climb down alone on no food too . . . but I still do not feel triumph or victory. It is too big, there is too much of it I would not dare set foot on.

Its cliffs are golden in the late afternoon sun. But mostly I feel it has earned its name: El Picacho del Diablo, Big Mountain of the Devil.

I am glad I'm not on the mountain—though if I were they would surely have found me by now. If I am to die, better here than on the mountain.

The direction of the wind has changed. The silver plane circles back and forth, back and forth above me. Hemlock burns with a fragrant smoke.

I admit it would be hard to take—to die here after having help so close above me. I'd continually be saying, "Oh if *I* had only done *this*, if *they* had only done *that*."

Patience ... *No!* ... I want to live, passionately, but if I have to die, I guess I'll learn to take it.

And Ogden ... it's torture not to know where he is, and whether he's alive. I am convinced he must still be on the mountain, and I pray they find him before it is too late.

If we both make it, future hardships will be relatively nothing, and hunger—God knows we would fervently be thankful for a daily diet of cornmeal.

If he is dead ... I might quit school, go to Vietnam as a Quaker refugee worker. I must do something that takes all my energy and devotion. I know that.

Or perhaps I'll study like mad and get my B.A. and be a social worker, knowing what it is to be hungry and have those you love in danger and dying. And someday I'll marry I suppose. But my husband will never know he married a ghost, and at night I'll walk the mountain in my dreams, and the cold wind will blow through the rags of my love forever.

Was it he I was calling to yesterday? "Help!" he called; "Hellooooo," and "Help!" I answered.

I suppose we'll be in the newspapers, whether we live or die. They'll say we are so stupid. So we are.

I will not think of death. Or perhaps I must.

Read Walt Whitman's "Out of the Cradle Endlessly Rocking." Read it. I shall.

When I run out of pages, write in the margins. I must write. Signing off for tonight—dark now. Wish I could sleep by the fire, but there's no place, too rocky. I can still hear the planes, but I can't see them. Not so cold tonight, little wind.

What day is this, anyway? Monday ... it's the third week of the new semester. So I've been missing two weeks. About time a search started.

Oh my empty stomach ... it growls and aches and water won't fill it.

◆

Journal of Francis Dart
SUNDAY, FEBRUARY 26
DRY LAKE EAST OF EL PICACHO

It has been a day of tremendous activity—too much to take in all at once. I got up not long after daylight and someone gave me some breakfast. The planned ascent of the mountain was called off, at least for now (I don't know why). Instead a group left at daybreak to go as far as possible up Diablito Canyon, Bernhard going with them but planning to come out in time to go up with the helicopter if it comes.

Ray dispatched a crew of trackers to run a complete arc through the desert from the southern ridge of the mountain south of Providencia all the way around and back to the mountain north of Diablo, just in case they came down on this side and went out into the desert.

Steve went with one of the Mexican police units to look into a canyon far to the south through which one can cross over the range to the west.

About 8:30 we got a message that two Navy helicopters coming from San Diego will be here at 9:30. They will have less than two hours of effective flying time here. I drove with Gill to the mouth of Diablito to pick up Bud and bring him back to meet them. We waited quite a while and watched one of the helicopters come before Bud finally showed up about forty-five minutes later than planned. He was sympathetic, still determined, but visibly depressed, telling me that everything indicated that they tried to scale the peak from this canyon. It is clear to me that he does not think they could make it.

He had stayed longer in order to search the trail and a camp up there more thoroughly—brought back a piece of Tampax and pieces of a dehydrated food envelope. More evidence that it is their tracks heading up this canyon.

We hurried out to base camp, meeting the tracking team from the north end of the valley who have followed them twenty-two miles across the desert and right into Diablito Canyon. They report that both hikers were strong and in good shape all the way.

At the lake bed we found a ferment of activity. One helicopter was already on its way to the summit. Another was waiting to take off. All around are small planes, jeeps, searchers, pilots, newspaper reporters, television cameramen, etc.

After a hurried conference with Bernhard, Ray decided to send the second chopper to search the ridge they must have tried to climb and to put some men up on that ridge. It went off at once with Bud and several of the Sierra Madre group. The rest of us were left to wait and watch.

It must have been very windy and turbulent at the summit. Through binoculars I watched the first helicopter make repeated passes trying to reach the summits—it looked somewhat like a mosquito hovering in an unsteady draft—and finally it held close enough for a man to jump to the north summit. This was repeated at the south summit, and then the delicate business of getting these men back by rope and winch was successfully carried out. A very dangerous and skillful operation that those of us on the ground watched with interest and apprehension. To some at least, it must have seemed a needless risk, for after Bud's report few expected that anything would be found in the register.

Finally the bird settled down on our lake bed and our little paramedic climbed out with an electrifying report. *They made it.* They signed the register on the north summit. One could feel almost a cheer go up as the news spread. A sense of admiration replacing the depression of a few minutes earlier.

But where are they? They signed the north summit register in good spirits ". . . the most spectacular climb I have ever made. . . ." It was not dated. They did not sign the register at the south summit, separated from the north by a technically difficult traverse along a very sheer ridge. The choppers had barely time enough left to make one more trip up. One was hastily dispatched to search the ridge separating the two summits and the cliffs below this ridge. The other was sent to search the upper part of Diablo Canyon, which is normally crossed in order to go over to the west.

More waiting until they returned to report nothing. No trace at all. The first even put down at a dry lake on the west side to look for tracks—nothing.

Then the helicopters left. They accomplished in less than two hours what would have taken days to do, and they brought us a lot of information but no solution. A conference now seems to indicate that the search must soon shift to the west side of the mountain. The trackers are back from the perimeter in the desert. Nothing. The men in the canyons are on their way out. Others here are packing up their gear to leave.

We have been in touch by plane on and off with the people on the west side who are approaching the mountain by trail. Norman flew in late in the afternoon after dropping them a message to say Eleanor and Ogden had reached the north summit. He reported that the search party was now on the plateau just west of the mountain and wanted water.

This information struck fire in the paramedic who ran over to confer with Bud. Both had seen smoke at "Blue Bottle" on the ridge west of the summits but had attributed it to the western search party, who now appear to be several hours short of there.

A frantic rush followed to get a plane up there before dark. Sergeant Morse of the San Diego Sheriff's office had gone to San Felipe for fuel and was not back yet. The other San Diego Sheriff's Patrol plane had only about thirty minutes of fuel left, but he took off anyway with Bud to look closely at Blue Bottle. Others began preparing to drop a radio by parachute for the ground party on the western meadows, along with instructions to push at once for that area and a query whether the smoke could have come from any of their party.

I sat apart in the Land Rover trying to find some inward quiet. This could be the break. They could be camped there and signalling for help. I pray it is true and wish I could be in the plane up there. After an incredibly long suspense the little plane returns. There definitely has been a fire there sometime recently, but there is no sign of anyone there now. In some way it still could have been their signal, but in my heart I know they are not there. If they were on Blue Bottle four hours ago they would not be strong enough at this date to leave.

We will still drop the radio and note to the climbers on the plateau. They can reach that area before noon tomorrow. Bud is impatient to get going even before we have put more fuel in the plane from our cans of spare automobile gas. He is impulsive and always impatient to get on with it—more impulse than judgment perhaps. He has amazing energy and determination. He is convinced now that they are up there and is planning to fly over to the Meling ranch, take a horse and start for Blue Bottle.

Darkness is approaching and the dry lake bed is almost deserted again. The planes and most of the vehicles are gone, and the base camp has packed up and gone, leaving behind nothing but a criss-cross of tracks in the sand. Most have returned home. Some have flown over to the Meling ranch to join the search on the west side. One group of climbers has not yet gotten out of Diablo Canyon, and some of their companions have gone to the end of the road to meet them. Ogden, Sr.'s brother will camp here and drive around to the west side tomorrow. Ray, too, is here waiting for the last party to get out.

I am waiting for Leonard and Gill, who took the two Indians back home somewhere beyond Trinidad—quite a long way I think. I have now a small collection of mementos picked up along their trail. Two or three dehydrated food wrappers—French's soup—a piece of Kleenex, a piece of plastic bag, and from far up Diablito Canyon on the side of the mountain itself, a piece of an envelope with the words "Eleanor Dart . . . from Jeanne" written on it.

These traces of my daughter and nothing more.

There are a few places still to search. There is hope still—there has to be hope. But I feel that we have failed and will not find them in time. Yes, I still hope, but I am coming to know the difference between hoping and expecting. I no longer expect to see Eleanor again.

I don't understand why, but somehow, in spite of everything, I have a strong feeling that everything is right, that with her, if not for us, it is good. Maybe it is the tone of her entry in the register—so happy and exuberant—maybe this is the way God tells me that His way is the right way. I don't know. I dread going back home to Alice and Paul. But soon I must. And somehow I will have to tell them that I failed, but that in some way Eleanor did not, or God did not.

9

Letting Go

From the Journal of Eleanor Dart

Morning clear, no visible sign of helicopters yet. Noises I can count on—these days every sound I hear is a plane for me. Should bathe—too tired. Wobbly walking, stumble easily. Oh where are the helicopters that will someday search this valley please?

Couldn't sleep, thought all night about food, every conceivable kind, and marriage. Clear night with stars.

My days are one long aching desire to be found, and my nights are one long aching desire for Ogden to be found, and for food.

Take cows now, cows are vegetarians and they are pretty meaty creatures. Of course, grain has lots of protein, and cows have two stomachs—makes it easier. Or rabbits ... now there's a meaty vegetarian for you. Or fish ... *lots* of fish ... no, there's insects for fish.

Why these ruminations? Well, I began the day in despair. All helicopter sounds are river sounds, emotion told me, and the search is over. I lay in my bag, contemplating my weakened state. WOE. It's hard to express my real misery, but it is *bad* when it comes.

Finally I sang a song to myself, always cheering—*I hear a plane, I know I do*—and decided to drag myself down to the creek and wash. I sat in the sun weakly testing the icy water with my toes and looking at the algae.

Well, why not? So I began to forage and spent a really very pleasant morning collecting and eating odd bits of vegetable matter and wading in the cool water—I'm quite refreshed by it.

I have got dark green, bulbous, slightly rubbery algae scraped from the underside of rocks. Not bad . . . utterly tasteless though. Long fiber-thin slimy strands of bright green algae, like spinach, only softer. Also tasteless. Longish stems with a reddish tint, quite juicy, with a fresh grassy flavor, fibrous unless very young. The leaves are slightly bitter and are furled like cabbage. Another has univalve leaves around a center like skunk cabbage and a tubular bulbous stem, bitter a little.

Finally I gathered some willow blooms. Quite a salad, no? It takes a long time to eat it. I can only get down a little at a time, and all must be carefully chewed—I do *not* have two stomachs—but I'm working on it. I lick my one remaining salt tablet intermittently for flavor. I wonder how long one could live on such stuff. I trust I won't poison myself . . . but I'm getting a headache, so perhaps I'd better hold off for a few hours just to see if I become violently ill. How will I know which plant did it?

Correction: my spirits fluctuate with (1) helicopters, (2) weather, and (3) activity.

Now I'm going to take a nap in the sun.

LATER

The sun went down, so I curled up in my sleeping bag. I thought for a while about all of the people I know who have been so kind to me, and how I love them so much. I felt that with so many people loving me I could not die. Eugene Friends Meeting,

Aunt Kay, the Ureys, the Pinneys ... I thought especially about the Pinneys and how I can never repay their kindness in making me a part of their family my first year away from home. I remembered swimming at night in the pool and playing with Julie. Dottie Pinney in her pink bathrobe in the kitchen making popcorn. I remembered a small softly lighted bedroom and puppies and pumpkin pie.

As the afternoon went on, I got into a sort of desperate state of mind. I am so alone here—my hope seemed gone. Somehow I managed to cling to my sanity by thinking about the Pinneys, concentrating on their kindness to me.

Later on I simply banished all thought of Ogden and rescue, and "If only we had," and death (*danger words ... get off of them*) by deciding to think about the past, and I worked myself into a sort of dreamlike trance thinking about Woodstock, the boarding school I went to in India, in a steady monologue, which I continued into the night. I shall have to do this quite often I think. I have had a fantastically varied life and there is plenty to reminisce about. I've never really thought much about my past before.

It strikes me now how incredibly regimented we were at Woodstock. Every day outlined rigidly in bells and hours. And we never questioned it. You knew just what would happen when, and the people and ideas made up the variety. I weep when I think of all the food I passed up and how fussy I was. . . .

So I thought through the night.

Remember essences ... warm pavement smells on a windy afternoon in Champaign, Illinois, and me in a Brownie uniform going down a long sidewalk to somewhere. . . . Burning leaves of fall, scuffing through brown-yellow ones on the sidewalks. . . . Halloween costumes whipped together by Mama on the morning of the day. . . . A present of homemade candy in the hospital in India when Mama, Helen and I had typhoid, and how we hoarded it, saving a piece to be the high point of each day.

Katmandu, Nepal—playing on the sunny dikes of the rice paddies and coming in for a glass of orange crush. And teatime at Woodstock—sandwiches (cucumber, tomato, potted meat, peanut butter, all thick and damp) and dark brown Indian tea with milk in it, and mail time.

Remember after tea our cannisters were set out and we could help ourselves to whatever our parents had sent us from home— Oreos, Ritz Crackers, sardines. And Saturday the candy man came and we bought chocolate bars and turkey eggs, English toffees and bull's eyes.

Sometime during the night I decided to believe that they have sent a search party up the canyon and eventually they'll reach me.

I refuse to believe that they have given up.

TUESDAY, FEBRUARY 28

It's easy to tell myself such things at night, but during the day when the sky remains empty, and no sounds can be heard except bird song and rushing water, it's much harder. Easiest to crawl into a hole like the dormouse, close one's eyes tight, shut out the world, and dream. But I can't do that all the time.

I try not to think of death 'cause I get panicky and sick inside, but I can't avoid the thought forever. It is always lurking. Patience, a game of Death's Head Patience. What shall I do? I have no patience. I couldn't wait—I had to keep moving. That's why I am dying now.

Again I think of trying to walk down the canyon. Why? I'm dizzy when I stand up. It takes me ten minutes to go fifty feet *without* a pack. How long is this canyon? How hard? What about the waterfall?

I say to myself, "Well, if I get stuck I am no more stuck than I am now." But probably the same thing will happen—they will finally look here, and I won't be here anymore.

Can I go a mile a day? And the desert—twenty miles of desert? Crazy, insane, and yet I may try it. Oh dear, hiking makes my stomach upset. But what else can I do? Shall I wait here one more day at least? Yes. But every day I get weaker. Already it's eighteen days without food.

Well, maybe I'll try it; I am what I am. At least I'll see new vistas on the way. *Oh, for a nice plate of enchiladas*. There's the old "die trying" Eleanor again. I don't trust her anymore, but I can't seem to deny her. She is.

Maybe there are fish lower down. I wonder if I can eat boot leather. Moccasins, I mean. I'll try.

Having decided on action, I felt better immediately and was sure that after all the rescuers would find me. I decided to sunbathe, so I went down by the creek. The effort literally made me breathless, and I realize, once and for all, that I physically *can not* hike out of here. I must give myself up to the unknown powers. I just plain am helpless. The decision is no longer mine, and as I did at Woodstock I must relinquish all control and simply obey.

A curiously peaceful realization, like when I had typhoid—I just had to let go and let myself be taken care of. It is very like that too. I remember what a tremendous effort it was to reach for a drink of water—just sitting up and pouring it—and that combing my hair was an exhausting major project. It's the same now. Everything is very tiring; any small effort seems enormous.

I feel happy. All I want to do is lie in the sun, and that is all I have to do. By the creek I saw tiny curled purple leaves, and a butterfly, a small blue butterfly with yellow wings.

I decided to bathe, so I stripped and looked at my body. I am really thin. My pelvic bones protrude, breasts almost gone, and I have no stomach at all. Emaciated but beautiful, golden-tanned and lithe. Hips still there, sigh, like a bushman. I squatted on a rock and washed. It felt good to have the sun dry me.

My shadow on the pebbled stream bottom was liquid and ripply, a lovely thing. I lay naked in the sun, peaceful, having given myself up to fate and faith.

Strange how moods come and go. One moment I am peaceful, the next I am terribly afraid, then in agony over mistakes made. I'll be afraid again, I know. Doubt and uncertainty are very hard for me to bear. But each fear will pass somehow, and there will be moments of peace like this. I needn't dwell on the thoughts that terrify me, although I can't always avoid them. As I get weaker I am more able just to lie in the sun and be.

I feel that Ogden is dead and we will never meet again. I am sure (*nothing is sure*), and I remember our parting and the gesture of peace he made to me. I know he has a harder burden to bear, up there on the mountain. And still, perhaps he is better equipped to bear it than I, if he still lives.

I know that I let him go to his death and that the burden of guilt for all of this is more mine than his. For his error was naivete and optimism, an *ignorance* of mountains, while mine was stupidity. I am a better mountaineer than he; I should have known not to make the mistakes I made—not to climb on when we should have turned back, not to let Ogden leave without the rope—but I made them and so may have killed us both. For a while it was an agony to bear, but I have come to accept this too. What is, is. What was, cannot be changed now.

Late today a silver plane circled the mountain three times and then left, and I thought the perhaps helicopter noises I had heard steadily droning above me all day ceased for a while, then started again more fitfully. What does it mean? Perhaps it means Ogden is found and they are getting him off the mountain. The location is about right. Perhaps not. I dare not speculate too much.

Whatever else it means, it means there is still something happening up there, and that is encouraging. Cold breeze now.

◆

Journal of Francis Dart
MONDAY, FEBRUARY 27
CLAREMONT, CALIFORNIA

This morning Leonard and I were up fairly early and after taking leave of Gill drove north through the desert toward Mexicali. The desert is very dry and looks barren when seen as a whole, but seen in smaller units it is alive and ready for spring. Purple flowers are blooming beside the road. A cactus with long slender stems, tufts of red flowers at their tips, and most plants have tiny green buds or new stems ready to start.

I like the desert best in early morning when the air is quite cool, and the mountains, still violet in the distance, are sharply etched against the sky. Fantastic mirages loom up. A hill towers three times too high, changes into a mushroom-shaped plateau of slowly shifting color and form, as though painted on a rubber backdrop that is now unevenly stretched upward. An island normally scarcely visible over the horizon stands high and clear, in the sky almost, but not quite disassociated from its roots in the sea.

Later, as the sun's heat reaches the desert floor, these images are replaced by their inverse, and where now we see land in the sky, we then see sky on the land, reflected from great pools of water that aren't really there. Before this change, the rising sun tints every peak and rocky hillside in rose and then in gold, and there is a brief interval of stillness and beauty that shares the coolness of the night with the warm light of the day.

We stopped for lunch in Calexico and were back in Claremont by late afternoon. Meanwhile nothing new has happened. Sgt. Morse has called a meeting of the principal people concerned at the San Diego Sheriff's office tomorrow evening to discuss the whole situation and decide what to do next.

During the morning I talked with Mother and a few others and sorted out the clothing and camp gear, packing mine up to be ready to go back to Mexico or back home, depending on the outcome of tonight's meeting. On the phone Alice sounds very tired. I think I should go back to her now, unless there is something I can do here, but it is so hard to know.

This afternoon Leonard and I drove to La Jolla where we met Ogden, Sr.'s father at the La Jolla Beach and Tennis Club, which he manages and owns. He told us that Ogden, Sr., is somewhere on the west side trying to follow up a signal seen from one of the planes. A note dropped at an isolated ranch house asking if the rancher had any information about two lost hikers produced an affirmative reply. This was some distance south of the Meling ranch.

We had dinner with the senior Kelloggs (grandparents of Ogden, Jr.) and their other son, and then went with them to the sheriff's office in San Diego. At the meeting Sgt. Morse carefully reviewed what has been done.

On the east side of the mountain, the only of all likely places that have not been searched are the uppermost portions of Diablo Canyon and of Providencia Canyon. Bud Bernhard is on his way down Diablo now. He is alone but has a radio and supplies. Morse is in touch with him from a plane once or twice a day. Providencia is not likely, but they could have tried to descend that way.

To the west, the meadows, Blue Bottle, and all the main approaches have been looked at, and two cowboys on horses are running a perimeter around the entire east side. So far no trace of any kind has been picked up anywhere on that side. All of the mountaineers except Bernhard have left or are on their way out.

Ogden will call this evening from Ensenada if they discover any clue at the ranch he is trying to reach.

We discussed additional things that can be done and decided to charter a helicopter to look again at the upper canyons and along the ascents from Diablo up to the meadows. It can in a short time also check out all the ranches directly. Mr. Harkness knows a competent pilot who has the right sort of machine, and he will try to arrange for this. I think this is a good idea, but it will be our last hope over most of the area, and we *must* have adequate support and back-up people with it.

Nothing was said about what to do after these plans. Everyone wants to think that each stage will be the last, but I suppose that all of us must privately concede that it may not be. I know that we must stop asking these people to risk their own safety as soon as we are sure that it is futile. But without actually finding them how can anyone be sure? How can anyone risk being mistaken? Even these men who have never even met Eleanor or Ogden cannot easily take that risk, for there is something more to it than just searching for someone's daughter or son who is lost. Somehow something of humanity itself is lost in their being lost, and even men who would have no reason to grieve at their death cannot be indifferent while they might be still alive. I think this is why a whole community will mobilize itself for a single child who falls into a well or is lost in a woods.

Nevertheless it must end sometime. Somewhere there is a divide beyond which we are no longer searching for the living but for the dead. There, if we could know where that divide is, we ought to stop, for I think there is something corrosive about searching for the dead. It takes too much away from the living even in ourselves. I feel that we are near to that divide already, but I don't know. And I don't know what is beyond.

I do know that I am not being useful here and I probably can't be. All the rules say I should stay and tomorrow go back to

Mexico and search more or get in the way more. I want to. But I know that Alice and Paul need help too and will soon need it more. I should and I will go there, at least for now.

I was up early to catch a plane from Ontario to San Francisco and then to Eugene. A bleak ride like a gray winter morning, or perhaps the ride was all right and the bleakness only in me. We have been surrounded by kindness and compassion everywhere. In Claremont as well as in Eugene—even at the airport as I arrived—and I am very grateful for it.

The bleakness is in me, I know, and it makes a sort of numbness. How can I tell Alice and Paul that Eleanor is gone and at the same time say that something about it, for her, is good? I don't even understand it myself. But I think it is true.

I keep remembering the last lines of her latest letter: "Ogden and I will be hitchhiking over semester break. I'm no fool, Mama, and I won't get killed on a mountain nor on the road."

Alice met me and brought me home for some lunch. Then I told her and Paul and Mother as much as I could about the search and about the next hopes. I also told them, or tried to tell them, how little hope there is now, and what I have come to feel about it.

I agreed to an interview with Don Bishoff of the *Eugene Register Guard*, but I didn't think I could face a television camera just now. Then I talked with Helen by phone.

Don Bishoff came and I answered his questions. I don't remember what I said.

10

A Gray Man

From the Journal of Eleanor Dart

I woke with the sun and didn't want to get up at all. I was too tired . . . almost exasperated. "Nothing will happen today," I thought, "another long day of nothing." Finally I rose to my feet, bedraggled and dirty, just to prove that I still could, and started to put on my scarf, when suddenly, "HOOOOO!" A loud cry, not twenty feet away.

I almost jumped out of my skin.

I had a vision of Og bounding out of the brush in robust health. "Hoo!" is his call.

"Hoo-oo-oo?" I called back, shakily.

"DART?" the voice called.

I came out into the clearing and saw a gray man, grizzled, bearded, covered with dust . . . a man. Alive. A human being.

"Oh my," I said. "Thank God."

He dropped his pack. "Drink this," he said, and gave me a can

of tomato juice. I was shaking so bad I had to sit down, almost
sick. We were both almost crying.

"I'm Bud Bernhard," he said. He was so shaken, like he
wanted to grab me and laugh and cry. He said he was the only
searcher still looking. He had radio contact with a plane once a
day—the same one I'd seen circle overhead three times yesterday.
He'd come down from the plateau on a hunch that someone had
to be in upper Diablo Canyon. He'd seen no one for a week.

He'd found my tracks last night and had been following them
on his hands and knees this morning when he came upon my
gold and silver paper markers and knew that someone, alive or
dead, was over that rock.

"Have they found Ogden?"

"No."

So I told him about the calling I'd heard and about the route
Ogden had taken. I said I was sure Ogden was still alive and I
thought I knew where. We drew maps in the dust. He wanted to
get it all straight before his plane contact came over. He was
moving around erratically, shaking. So was I.

He gave me cookies and I ate them. Food after eighteen days
of water.

He started getting my gear together and said I was well
equipped. Then his plane flew over.

The radio wouldn't work. Pretty soon the plane flew away.
There was no help for it—we decided to start hiking out down
Diablo Canyon. If the plane didn't come back today, it would
come tomorrow.

Bud took everything heavy and put little things in my pack.
We wrapped my Walt Whitman in plastic and left him for someone to find someday, and then set out.

It was very hard at first. Bud was so careful of me. He checked
out the route ahead at every point. He wouldn't let me go *one
step* higher or farther than I needed to. But it was pretty hard. I
was so tired. I had to rest often and my stomach felt sick and my

head got all full and hot and dizzy. But I kept going. I had to. I had to get out so that they could go in and find Ogden. The radio contact had failed, so we had to carry the news out on foot.

It was an agony we both shared. I'd explained carefully to Bud just where I thought Ogden had to be. I knew he'd been alive five days ago, but we both knew it could be a matter of hours how long he'd live if he still were alive.

Bud wanted to take my rope, turn on his heel and go rope up that canyon alone to find him. I desperately wanted him to go, but we both knew that until someone else knew I was alive he couldn't leave me. If he got killed, then I would die too.

It was an agony, but we had to walk away from Ogden, down the canyon. The radio, why hadn't it worked? We prayed for the plane to return. I didn't think it would. I know those empty skies—they don't divulge planes lightly.

After a while Bud gave me a can of Sego and it really hit the spot—cool and sweet like a vanilla milkshake. He was so glad I liked it. He had five cans he'd been saving for me, or for Ogden, in case. After I drank that I began to move pretty fast. He kept saying, "Do you realize how bitchin' you're going?"

We were in a red-walled rocky section of the canyon, in shade at last, when I heard the plane. We dropped our packs and tore his open with frantic haste, got out the radio and the antenna . . . it worked.

I lay down on the ground and cried and sobbed while he told the plane he'd found me, I was in poor condition, he wanted four strong rock climbers to come up with him to look for Ogden, and a relief party to help me get down the canyon. He and I would proceed down and meet them.

I wept.

I felt so much relief, such sudden hope that Ogden would be found too. Let him be alive, please, let him be alive.

We were high on adrenaline then and began to move pretty fast. It is a spectacular canyon—red walls, striated patterns in the riverbed, clear flowing water. At one place we found a smooth natural slide into a scooped-out hollow—we thought about swimming but decided to wait and wash at evening.

We hiked until the late afternoon light began to make the upper canyon a tawny rose. We got below the big bend in the canyon, where it turns to cut through the mountain itself toward the desert. There the terrain changed abruptly from pine trees and ferns to sandy desert, Spanish bayonets and cactus.

We camped under low trees beside the water. I was so tired. We washed, built a small fire and soaked beef jerky to make broth. I ate the beef and the broth and another can of Sego. Bud gave me all his food and I gave him my toothbrush.

Suddenly Bud's plane was overhead, then another, then a huge helicopter, flying low. They wanted to drop food or airlift me out or something. Bud had called my condition poor instead of fair and they thought I was near death.

Bud refused to signal to them. He was furious and upset. He said the canyon winds made it very dangerous to land a big helicopter. Someone would get killed for sure.

I thought that if Ogden was alive, at least all the commotion would assure him that something was still happening. It makes so much difference just to know someone is looking for you. When you believe they have given up, you are terribly alone. I had a sort of a funny fear that Ogden might give up and decide to die.

Bud talked to his plane. He said I was doing fine, the most wonderful girl in the world, eating all his food and he was going hungry and loving it. He said I'd heard Ogden calling, but that was five days ago, and Ogden, Sr., probably must try to accept the idea that we might have to carry his son's body out. That was hard to hear. Very hard.

Finally everything quieted down. Bud and I talked for a while as the stars came out.

There was a strong silent bond between us. This man whom I had never met before, who had been looking for me for weeks, always believing I was there, convinced by my father's certainty, refusing to give up. (I had tried so hard to call to Daddy, "I'm here. I'm here.") I who had been waiting so long for someone to come. We didn't need words, we were both so used to silence.

It was peaceful in the canyon. So many stars. I played taps on my harmonica, and we went to sleep.

I woke several times in the night. The moonlight was brilliant on the canyon walls, and I heard some little animal rustling in the leaves near our camp. It was hard to sleep. I was thinking about Ogden a lot. I wanted him to be alive so much. In a deep concentrating faith somehow I knew that he was alive, that he must be saved. And still I was comfortable and warm and fed and safe myself. That was good.

The real suffering is never just physical.

THURSDAY, MARCH 2

I woke when the first golden light of dawn was touching the upper canyon walls and lay in my sleeping bag feeling very peaceful. Sunlight and birds calling. Sweet day, the water singing in the stream. It felt so good to be alive.

After a while Bud woke up too and gave me a can of Sego.

Suddenly a tiny helicopter appeared out of nowhere, like a noisy glass bubble, and began to circle our camp. I felt like hiding. Bud erupted again about canyon winds and danger. The truth is we were both angry because our peace was shattered. The strange small world of rescuer and rescued was coming to an end.

The helicopter wouldn't leave. It dropped off a man who talked to Bud and then absconded with his radio. The man told Bud that no one was at the canyon mouth yet. Bud was furious. He decided to go back and look for Ogden himself, so I gave him my first-aid gear, rope, prussiks, all the food and my little bottle of wine, which I'd not ever gotten desperate enough to drink.

Then three men appeared and things began to straighten out. This little chopper could put a man down almost anywhere. It would take me out to the dry lake where a new base camp of rescuers was forming, and then come back and set Bud down on the mountain near where he and I thought Ogden had to be.

We hiked to where they'd left it and I climbed in. Such a crazy tiny bird. We rose up and followed the canyon close to the rocky walls. I sang to myself to keep from getting too excited. We landed on the dry lake and a strange man helped me out. "I'm Ogden," he said, and I recognized Ogden's father and just held on to him.

Right away I told Ogden, Sr., everything I knew about Og's route and his plans, where I'd heard him, that I *knew* I'd heard him, it had to be him, and he'd been alive. Then there was nothing to do but wait.

It is very hard, this waiting. Ogden, Sr., had been waiting like that for three weeks. Not knowing. Never knowing.

The camp was a bustle of orange-coated men from the Sierra Madre Search and Rescue Group—a crack organization with all kinds of communications set up—airplanes, and newspapermen.

A man named Charles Kassler gave me an old beat-up Hershey bar and some M&M's chocolate-covered peanuts. He said his kids saved their Halloween candy for the Search and Rescue group to give to found people. He had the kindest blue eyes and most wonderful smile.

I talked to a lot of newsmen. I changed into my dress. Pretty soon we heard that Bud had been put down on the mountain above Cold Slot Wash. I ought to explain that. Below the innocent-looking rock slide that Ogden set out to climb down is a sheer drop of 2,000 feet. That is Cold Slot Wash. There is a route down it if you traverse way to the left, but I figured Ogden got stuck somewhere and couldn't go on or go back.

They decided to take me up in the chopper to trace his probable route down from where he'd left me. By now they had a sort of heliport in the canyon and we flew there first. They set off a bright orange flare as we landed. The pilot got out and all the men grabbed him and started yelling.

I couldn't hear. I didn't dare believe anything. I waited. The pilot got back in and we took off.

He said, "Well, they've found your boyfriend. He's alive."

I began to cry. I rocked back and forth and wailed for joy.

They took me back to the dry lake and there was Ogden, Sr., and we held on to each other and cried. After all these nights of praying and believing, to have him alive. . . .

The chopper pilot had flown Bud over the area and Bud told him exactly where to set him down. "There," he said. Later he said, "It had to be there. There was no time to make mistakes."

He was set down only 150 feet above the small hidden ledge where Ogden was lying, and had been lying for two weeks.

Ogden said he saw the chopper, knowing it couldn't see him, then thought he heard a voice. He yelled.

"He had a heck of a voice," said Bud. "It shook the canyon."

They yelled back and forth and Bud worked his way down as close to Ogden as he could get, then tried to lower him food. The first two cans missed the ledge. Ogden said, "Wrap it in your shirt," and the next one got to him. I think it was beans. Ogden loves beans.

Later, when they were setting up the ropes to raise him 350 feet over an overhang to where the chopper could pick him up, Bud made them take him my little bottle of wine. "A present from your wife," they said. He drank it. He says it did him good.

There was a long wait at base camp while they got him off the mountain. It took all of the men the Sierra Madre group had there, except Ray, who stayed to work communications. I talked to him. He told me about how he and his brothers started the rescue group fifteen years ago.

"You two kids better do something worthwhile with your lives," he said.

Ogden, Sr., taught me a beautiful knot called the renda that Mexican cowboys use. I taught him a butterfly knot.

I talked to so many newsmen.

Mr. Harkness said his jeep was so full of smiles he figured he could fly it home.

I walked out alone across the dry lake. The ground was dusty and puckered under my feet, blue sky with wispy clouds blowing in a wind from somewhere, warm sunlight on the mountain. I lay down and listened to the silence and felt the wind. After a while Ogden, Sr., came over and sat beside me, and we talked quietly or sat in silence.

Finally, just after the sun dropped below the mountains, the little chopper came down with Ogden in it. He got out and hugged his father, and then I ran into his arms and for a minute we just held on to each other. Then Ogden, Sr., and I got him into the truck and shut the door on the reporters. He was dazed, bewildered, very weak.

He was so thin. The bones in his face showed up under a month's growth of beard, and he had tiny chicken feathers all through his hair and sweater from a leak in his sleeping bag. He told us what happened to him.

Forty-five minutes after he left me on the ridge he was stuck, and he stayed there for two weeks. He was climbing down a crack at the top of Cold Slot Wash. (How many times after he left me had I agonized because I didn't say to him, "Ogden, don't go down anything you can't come up.") He got jammed in the crack with his pack.

He had to get the pack off, got out of one strap but couldn't get out of the other. He was terribly afraid. Finally he sort of flipped around and got the pack off, but it fell and skittered down the rock to a little ledge about fifty feet below. Then Ogden fell and landed on the same ledge. It was about ten feet long and two feet wide with a waterfall hitting one end of it. Ogden couldn't climb back up and he didn't dare go on down. He was shaken and frightened: somehow he felt that the mountain was full of demons and out to get him. So he stayed right there.

The ledge was covered with snow. He spread out his tarp, foam pad and down bag on the snow and got in. Every day he'd get up in the morning to go to the bathroom and black out, fall down and get up again. Every day he'd go to the end of the ledge to fill his canteen at the waterfall. He was so dizzy that it frightened him, but he found he felt stronger when he drank a lot of water, so he did it.

There were little sparrows who had their nests in the rocks around him. He watched them flying and thought how ironic it was that this place, their haven of safety, was going to be his grave, for he believed he was going to die there.

Once an eagle perched above him and he watched it. One night it rained and the waterfall came right down on top of him, soaking his bag completely. He sang Christmas carols and pretended it was snowing, but he never got warm again. He only saw the sun for five minutes on the last day he was there. He got used to the idea that the planes and helicopters couldn't see him. Most of the time he'd dream or think about food. He said he thought about every meal he ever ate.

He said often in his dreams, almost every night, he and I would escape from the mountain together, always together, but he'd always left something behind, his body, and he couldn't get away.

In his dreams the dream people would tell him, "This is only a dream you know." And he'd say, "I know. I can't leave here. But maybe you can. Maybe you can tell someone I'm here."

The whole time he was terribly hungry. Starving. He believed he would starve to death there, and he thought I would run out of water and die up on the ridge. It did things to him, lying there alone with this for two weeks. He changed.

We left the dry lake in a small airplane. On the plane Ogden turned to me. "I'm not going to Canada," he said. "I want to join the American Friends Service Committee. I want to feed people." He said that if he'd died there, as his last act, he was going to cut his finger and write on the rock wall above him in blood, "Feed the millions."

We flew over the mountain into the sun. It was as if I had never seen the sun before. The light was total, filling all things like the first evening of the world. We landed at the Rancho San Jose.

A roast beef dinner, a blazing fire, champagne, people celebrating, cheering, laughing . . . but in my mind there was only Ogden's swollen feet, cold and black, his pain, the touch of our hands, the peace of no more struggle.

We went to bed in adjoining rooms with small fireplaces, firelight glowing warm on adobe walls. Someone gave me a rose-red bathrobe, and my whole memory of that night is rose-red and warm and full.

I lay between cool clean sheets, my mind clear at last, and slowly the past weeks opened to my spirit's eye. I saw a vision of the mountain and us on the mountain seen from high above that was like a hand pointing.

I know power now. Our strength is more than our own. I know that the ability to consent is a gift of grace. I did not attain it, it was given to me, and with it came deep peace.

After that night things began to happen very fast. It was hard for me. My whole being had changed tempo, slowed to match the timeless motion of rocks and trees. The mountain had become my reality.

11

God Does Not Forget

From the Journal of Francis Dart

Late this afternoon Leonard called to say Eleanor has been found. She is alive. She is in poor shape, he says, but she is alive. Bud Bernhard found her today and is with her, and more help is on the way. Ogden is not with her and has not been found yet. No other information.

Such overwhelming relief. We can hardly feel anything else it seems, although actually we do. Conviction, even certainty, that she'll be all right now, sympathy and worry for Marjorie Kellogg, even amusement at the newspaper photographer who wanted us to pose with the telephone and radiate joy while talking with our long lost daughter.

I for one know how few telephones there are in Diablo Canyon. And how can we feel joy with Ogden still lost?

THURSDAY, MARCH 2

Ogden was found today, alive but in worse shape than Eleanor, who is better off than was at first supposed. Both will be all right in the end, they say. I hope they'll both be taken out and to San Diego today.

A day of telephone calls and radio and newspaper reporters. We couldn't tell them much because we don't really know much. So we answer real questions as well as we can and silly questions as politely as we can.

We rejoice together. We can sleep tonight. I'll have to wait until later to understand everything in me.

FRIDAY, MARCH 3

Olin Byerly has flown Alice and Paul to Claremont in his plane. Eleanor and Ogden are in San Diego, he in a hospital with frozen feet, and she at the home of the senior Kelloggs, soon to leave for Claremont. There has been a lot of press, radio and TV coverage of the final stages of their rescue and evacuation.

Alone again—it seems as though I've been alone so much, although I haven't been really—I've tried to think about it all, but I can't yet. Too tired and relieved I suppose.

How I have wished I could be there to meet Eleanor as she came out, or to go to her in Diablo. I'm sure she will feel betrayed when I am not there. She won't be alone in that—I too feel that I have deserted her.

TUESDAY, MARCH 7
OVER THE PACIFIC EN ROUTE TO THAILAND

Friends Meeting in Eugene on Sunday was quiet and full of love and rejoicing. As the Meeting closed Gary Hubbe started singing the Beethoven "Alleluia" joined by all the rest of the

Hubbes. After lunch I packed up for Thailand and flew to Ontario, California, where Leonard met me.

I spent yesterday in Claremont with Eleanor. She read part of her diary to me and we told each other about our separate and yet strangely not-so-separate experiences. She appears tired but really quite well, everything considered, and seems to me to be more at peace than she has been in a long time. She has come to terms with something of herself and with God in more depth than before.

The opposite seems to be true of me, and I envy her the tranquility she has found. Trying to find what is troubling my soul, I thought at first it was merely disappointment that I couldn't be a part of the final rescue—and a bit of envy of those who could—but I find it is much more than this.

I'm nearly overwhelmed by the terrible responsibility we hold for each other. Another's life is a heavy load to hold in one's hands or in one's trust, and we hardly know when we may drop it without a thought really. Eleanor and I came so terribly close to doing just that last Christmas without even suspecting it. How many times have I really done so? "Not to know" is surely no excuse. God does not say: "Practice faith only when you know."

How can you "know" when to stop believing that a lost daughter will be found? You can't know. But without knowing anything, I gave up believing she was alive. I gave up and went home to persuade Alice to stop believing it too, *and all the time Eleanor was alive and needing us*. How could she forgive this? How can I?

I don't think that I will be able to forgive it and so I think I too will have been changed by this experience.

However much I lack in faith, though, God does not forget nor give up. He *was* with her all the time. I wouldn't have thought the San Felipe desert nor Diablo Canyon a likely setting for David's psalm,

The Lord is my shepherd,
I shall not want.
He maketh me to lie down
    in green pastures,
He leadeth me beside the still waters,
He restoreth my soul.

But it is.

DECEMBER 24, 1967
EUGENE, OREGON

A vivid dream came to me last night. No action in it and no face. Just a clear insistent quotation:

"Listen and do not forget, and I will show you a mystery. It is not the sacrifice, whether it comes in youth or age, or the god remits it; it is not the bloodletting that calls down power. It is the consenting, Theseus. The readiness is all. It washes the heart and mind from things of no account, and leaves them open to the god."

Only this, with a strong sense that it is speaking to me.

I lay awake a long time thinking about where this might come from and what it might mean. I know the quotation came from Mary Renault's *The King Must Die*, which I read months ago.

It seems to be saying, "Be at peace now. Consenting to God's way is no betrayal."

So much has happened these past months. It is hard to sort it all out in an orderly way, but I know most of it has been good, or will be. Yet consenting was not easy, not for me anyway.

Tonight will be Christmas Eve. Alice, Paul and I will be at home together. Eleanor and Ogden will be at home too—at his home.

Be at peace now.

12

This Is the Place

This is the story of how we begin to remember,
This is the powerful pulsing of love in the vein,
After the dream of falling and calling your name out,
These are the roots of rhythm,
And the roots of rhythm remain.

Paul Simon
"Under African Skies"

It is a spring morning in 1987. I am hanging out wash on the clothesline in the sun. The desert is full of birds building nests in the cholla cactus, flying in and out of saguaros with bits of twine and grass. My black lab Annie drops her stick on the clean clothes in the wicker basket to make sure I won't miss it. I throw it for her. Out in the pasture the horses are frisking about, chasing each other in short gallops.

A curve-billed thrasher lights on the red-tiled roof of the old ranch house and walks along the ridge. This is my first April in Tucson, Arizona.

I first set foot in Tucson two years ago. I stepped off the plane. I breathed the air. Around me stretched the Sonoran Desert. To the north, south, east and west rose mountains, rugged peaks of tumbled rock. I felt like a gong, struck and sounding. A long-forgotten chord of music began to echo through me—"This is the place."

Ten months later I pulled up stakes and headed south. As I drove east from Yuma and the desert opened before me, I felt as if, in an old spy movie, I was one piece of a postcard ripped in two long ago, and this landscape was the other half. I enter the Sonoran Desert and suddenly the torn edges match without a flaw. Some coded message held secret half my life is released. I cannot read the cipher yet, but I hold it in my hand.

The last years have been hard ones—a long painful battle with cancer, bankruptcy and divorce. In the months that follow I sink into the desert. For the first time in twenty years I am alone. I climb mountain ridges and sit for hours on rocks watching the weather move across the sky. I listen to hawks. Amber grasses sway. Many birds fly up from the bushes, singing.

Winter comes and storms blow into the valley from the western ocean. Great gusts of wind pierce my solid adobe walls with sound.

The bedroom is icy. I pull my mattress in front of the living room fireplace, make brief freezing dashes to the bathroom. Annie and I take long walks in the country air.

I'm living on the fringe. I never read the paper or watch the news. A friend says, "You've gotten off the train." The train roars on far away. I have no desire to get back on.

One spring morning, canyon-climbing on a smooth highway of water-polished granite, I come to a pool deep enough to be green. I strip, dive in, climb out with every nerve tingling and lie on the warm rock, drowsing. Annie plays with her stick—dropping it off the rocks into the pool, trying to reach it, falling in.

Something about the granite cliffs towering above me, the musical rushing of the water, the solitude . . . surely I have been here before. . . .

I begin to remember.

13

Lost

The sky is completely black and rain pours down. I lean into the wind and struggle up a hill I cannot see in the darkness. It is mid-winter in the small fishing town of Prince Rupert, British Columbia, 1969. Across the Tsimshian River on the edge of town rise the coastal mountains of Alaska. El Diablo is a distant memory. Ogden and I have been married two years.

That first year our off-campus house by the University of Oregon is a center for the Draft Resistance Movement. I make huge pots of soup and bake bread. AWOL GIs crash on our floor. I burn Ogden's draft card on the steps of the Student Union and make the front page of the *Eugene Register Guard*. Everyone says I am a tower of strength.

Late at night I am working alone in the pottery studio at the university. I pull a firebrick out of the kiln door and look in to see the incandescent shapes of pots glowing red-white in the fire. I kick the weighted wheel and feel cool gray clay turning between my palms. It is very quiet. I pull the clay up between my fingers to form the curved sides of bowls. My mind is completely empty. My body remembers what I have forgotten. This is real to me, only this.

The winter of 1968 is cold, two feet of snow on the ground in Eugene stop traffic for a week, and then the rains blow back in. Ted is living with us now, a stocky, red-bearded mountaineer. The three of us kayak the Willamette River in December, silently gliding over dark water in falling snow. Ogden drops out of school and he and Ted get jobs planting trees on a reforestation contract.

It is 4:00 A.M. Rain beats against the windows from the blackness outside. I am packing lunches of fresh scones and strong hot tea by candlelight. Ted watches me from his mattress in the living room. The attraction between us is so intense I can see it in the air, a vibrating, opalescent shape between our bodies as I bend to open the door of the wood stove, my arms full of split pine.

At 5:00 the two of them pull on their muddy boots and slam out into the storm. I lie beside the open stove, the cat and her seven kittens piled soft on my belly, daydreaming in the warm firelight.

Spring comes and Ogden is drafted. He refuses induction and we move into in the old cabin on his parents' farm. I dry corn in the sun, grinding kernels into meal for round sweet corn cakes. Ceramic vats of new milk ripen into yogurt in the kitchen. Ogden works the farm with his dad. They stack baled hay on a slow moving wagon, sweating in the still summer air. Fields of purple-blossomed alfalfa curve up to steep hills shimmering with live oak and madrone.

Ted has left to study wolves in Alaska. In the evenings Ogden and I read Gary Snyder's poetry aloud to each other by candlelight. Late one night I am awakened by piercing wails and a bubbling musical sobbing outside our bedroom window—it is a porcupine up in a tree, crying to the moon.

The call comes while we are at a Quaker workshop in British Columbia—the FBI have come to pick him up. Ogden decides he cannot face jail. We stay in Canada.

Now the war is winding down and so is the marriage. Outside the window of our bare apartment dark water streams down black cliffs. Ogden runs a forklift in a lumber mill; I work swing shift as a long-distance telephone operator. Ogden is depressed and homesick. I lie beside him in the bed at night, rigid with a rage I don't understand. I want to scream and kick him. The impulse is so strong that I know I will do it, and I move into the living room.

Christmas comes and I spend weeks carefully handmaking tree ornaments out of egg cartons, glitter and glue. I decorate Christmas cookies in the shapes of angels and doves. I make an Advent calendar, drawing tiny pictures with colored inks of shepherds and candy canes behind little cardboard windows. I tape the calendar in front of the dripping rocks and open one window every day. My mind is cracking.

I write to my father and he answers on the thin gray paper of air letters:

"I'm on my way home, looking down on the Lake Michigan shore—clean white sand and clear cold water in the sunshine. I was finishing high school or in college . . . golden summer days picking blueberries, watching birds . . . tanagers, gulls, terns. If there were troubles in my world, they could never reach me there. I wish I could have given you something like that to remember.

"Your life has been so different from mine. You used to say, 'But Daddy, you don't understand!' and of course you were right. I didn't and couldn't although I wanted to, still want to.

"One thing I do understand though: life is not all of one color. Not mine and not yours. Sometimes it is full, sometimes almost empty; sometimes bleak, sometimes gay. Often we can't be sure until later. You do have the intelligence and spirit to know finally what is right and you do have the strength then to do what is needed. When you know, then don't cling to indecision, and if you *must* gamble sometime then do it with a free spirit."

Finally we give it up. We take the long train ride south through the Rockies to Vancouver, cross the border, hitch the freeways home. Ogden turns himself in. He is declared 4-F because of his frozen feet and released. It is over.

It is 1970 and the vets are coming home. A man I am seeing shows me long twisted scars on his legs, pierced by sharpened bamboo stakes in a Viet Cong booby-trap. He buys a Harley and runs it under a truck. The Harley is totalled. He lives.

Og and I get divorced in 1972. Three years later I receive a postcard from somewhere in the Rockies. He has remarried, moved back to the farm, had a son.

I never see him again.

14

My Father Always Promised Me

The log cabin sits above a meadow looking out over the Ashland valley in southern Oregon. I have driven ten miles up Dead Indian Road and hiked two more on a steep twisting mud track to find this place. No one is around. Inside the cabin someone is screaming, "I hate you, I hate you!" I sit on a rock and wait.

The screaming stops, to be replaced by sobbing and then silence. After a while the cabin door opens and a few people straggle out into the sun. One of them is Sandy, the man I have come to see.

Sandy, a short, dynamic man with intense brown eyes, is an artist and self-styled therapist who retreated to these mountains from New York with his wife and two children. He built his cabin, worked in sculpture and drawing, and studied raccoons. A few art students from the college sought him out as a teacher, one thing led to another, and now he leads weekly groups. He is viewed with deep suspicion by much of Ashland. . . . "What goes on up there? Sexual orgies . . . ?" His students are a small, tight group of true believers who form their own community within the town.

Sandy and I talk briefly. He tells me I am very angry. I don't know if this is true, but I know I am unhappy, searching for something I cannot define.

We are refugees from the sixties, back from Canada, from Vietnam, from early doomed marriages, back from Freedom Marches in the South, back from rock concerts and the City of Love, back from acid trips where we tried to find ourselves and failed. We are in our twenties and early thirties, and our parents' lives are not our lives. It's not working. All over the country we are joining communes and keeping bees, eating brown rice, trying group marriage, raging and weeping in primal scream therapy or rolfing or EST, looking for something to believe in.

At night, lit by kerosene lamps, the cabin is dark, warm, womblike. The shared premise is that our parents failed to love us enough; we are children jerked out of paradise, deprived of our birthright as simple animals. We come here to be reborn.

Someone puts on music, Judy Collins singing "My father always promised me that we would live in France. . . ." and a dark-haired young woman takes the floor, crying, begins to dance.

"It's hard to be the daughter of a Quaker saint," my sister once said. In Sandy's classes I find plenty of reasons to hate my thoughtful, idealistic father. A noisy, impetuous child, it seemed I spent a lifetime trying and failing to meet his high standards. Under a barrage of group encounter tactics, I realize that my entire family is neurotic, sexually repressed, emotionally sterile. Perhaps my father can be healed with me . . . I write, asking him to come to a marathon weekend class.

"It's lovely of you to wish I would join you," he replies. "I accept in spirit . . . I probably won't in practice. . . ."

My mother writes, "Darling . . . Why should you have to engage in therapy? Is it not in the scheme of things that you could, bright-eyed and courageous, go on just to live, taking things as they come, and coping? You seem very whole to me. . . ."

It will be ten years before I realize that she is right.

I break off relations, stop writing, stop visiting. The class becomes my family. Christmas, Thanksgiving, New Year's, we celebrate at Sandy's cabin or at each other's houses. We have affairs with each other, live together, break up, intermarry. We start day-care centers and treatment programs and give poetry readings on campus. Every Saturday is spent in group therapy, often in forty-eight-hour marathon sessions, unburdening our souls.

I become an expert at weeping, raging, attacking, dancing with joyful abandon. Yet within the group I remain oddly isolated. Always I feel distant somewhere deep inside, even from the men I live with and believe I love. This must be my neurosis, mea culpa, and I keep trying, hoping to be healed.

One summer, Ernie, a Klamath River Indian newly released from doing time for manslaughter, comes to class. His arms are brown whorls of bunched muscle, the fury emanating from his taut body pushes us back against the cabin walls. This is real anger, and we quickly seek ways to tame him, to protect ourselves from too much reality.

On a June morning in 1973 I graduate from Southern Oregon State College. My parents come down for the ceremony. After hours of sweating in the sun on hard metal chairs, I meet Mama and Daddy and we walk up the hill above Lithia Park to my small rented house. My father is enormously proud of me and he tells me so. He gives me a small gold watch on a black velvet band.

I have fulfilled a dream for him. It means everything to me that he is here. I want to say to him, "Daddy, this is my gift to you. I know how much you love me. I love you too." But I am mute.

The letters keep coming. In 1976 I receive a letter in fine shaky handwriting with sentences that straggle across the page and fade out into faint ghosts of words. "I am sitting by the fire listening to the Beatles' song 'Once there was a way to get back home-ward,'" he writes. "I used to think there was a way. But no more. . . ." I know something is terribly wrong.

There is a tumor the size of a robin's egg growing behind my father's right ear, sending out thin tendrils into his brain. The cancer is inoperable. Within three months he is dead.

I do not cry when my father dies. I go to the funeral dry-eyed. It is as if a gauze curtain separates me from my life. I reach out to touch across a great distance, and can feel nothing.

15

One Joy at a Time

It is July in Tucson. A monsoon wind is blowing the curtains back from the eastern window of my bedroom, carrying the scent of rain.

Tears blind me, tears held back. I am exhausted from shoring up the dam. Finally I howl, pacing the floor, sobbing uncontrollably. This has been going on for weeks. I don't know why I am crying.

Some internal reservoir of heartbreak has cracked open and I am helpless in the flood. Tears well up in me without warning. From the library, the market, the bookstore I run for my car and drive around for hours, shaken with sobbing, pounding on the wheel. I don't understand it. I feel I cannot stand it. My arms and breast ache with emptiness, with the loss . . . of what? I do not know.

I call friends and they offer what comfort they can. A glass of wine. The touch of hands. They tell me about simple things— taking the kids to the park, rebuilding a jeep—and their voices are like soothing music. For a time I am calmed.

Then it hits me again. Grief grabs me with blunt teeth and shakes me head to toe. I begin to feel like a boxer in the tenth round of a losing fight. I keep getting knocked down, I struggle to my feet, and WHAM, I'm down again.

Now it is an August afternoon and despair has driven me from the house. The sky over the Santa Ritas south of Tucson is black as night. I turn the wheel and head into the storm.

Out Houghton Road the first drops hit the truck and then a torrent of rain engulfs me. I pull over and sit with windows open as rain crashes on the roof and blows in sheets into the cab. Fingers of lightning touch down all around me; thunder rips the sky over my head. Rain bounces off the pavement, and swift streams of water cut small gullies in the red-brown sand beside the road.

The wind is cool. I open the door and step out into the storm. Water pours over my skin. Lightning strikes again, and I jump for the car.

I drive for hours, chasing the rain. Out to the Santa Ritas, east toward Dragoon and El Paso. Gray clouds move across the sky, releasing long, traveling sheets of coolness.

Toward evening I find myself driving slowly home over the small hills of Old Spanish Trail. The sunset light is golden on the palo verdes. The desert smells of rain.

One morning high in the pines of the Catalinas a companion picks up a piece of granite studded with flakes of sparkling mica. "What kind of rock is this?" I answer and hear my father's voice patiently explaining how crystals grow.

Daddy seems to live within me in the days that follow— I feel his free-swinging stride as I walk; I sense his thoughts inside my mind. I begin re-reading the letters he wrote me, long buried in dusty boxes. The love in them is so intense that I can hardly bear it.

"I like the song: 'My father always promised me...,'" writes Daddy. "It invites one to weep for lost faith or lost dreams. I've had my share of them too. . . . But there is an answer contained in the song itself. 'My father always promised me that we would live in France. . . ,' and the singer herself now lives in France! The father didn't make it, I guess, but his daughter did, and now in her song she turns her nostalgia back toward the Ohio mining town.

"I think her father made it too. I think his promise and his aspirations were for her more than for himself. No doubt the mines held him and disappointed him too—but she made it. She lives in France. Joy for him.

"Speaking as a real father, what did *I* think I was promising you? That everything would be all right? In the end, yes. That dreams would be fulfilled? Yes, sometimes if not always, but not without effort. One thing I did used to say—so much that Mama used to tease me about it: 'It's hard, but you can do it.' Dreams are not made real easily. A faith or a life dies and is reborn with real pain. It *is* hard. But you can do it, and in the doing you can find both joy and excitement.

"I would love to climb a real mountain with you. I'm willing to try any pitch with you for which you are ready to say to *me*, 'It's hard, but you can make it.' Provided you are giving me the upper belay."

We never climbed that mountain. I turned away and then he was gone. And I could not forgive myself for abandoning him. I never mourned my father. His loss was too painful, my guilt too great. . . . I drew a veil over the past; I went numb. For years I have been blindly seeking absolution. Until now.

Now I am seeking with eyes open. I read Daddy's letters and the love there keeps breaking my heart. I walk into the pain, remembering.

Early on an October morning I am driving to Pontatoc Canyon in the Santa Catalina Mountains. Last night the first autumn storm swept through the valley and I fell asleep listening to wind and rain shuddering through the eucalyptus trees outside my window. This morning the skies are clear as spring water. Every leaf and stone is etched in brilliant light.

I leave the truck and hike up the canyon. Red- and gray-banded cliffs tower above me. Sand grits beneath the soles of my shoes.

The trail is alive with tiny red ants, working the ground after the rain. Birds flash by and land, lizards dart up the rocks. A few prickly pears still carry fat red fruits, weighting down the ends of their pads. In the creek bottom the cottonwoods have turned gold.

I push myself up the steep hillside enjoying the good feel of muscles working deep in my legs. Halfway to the ridge I stop, breathing hard, and turn to look out over the valley. The mountain is silent in the morning air.

I can see every rooftop of the city below, and beyond to Baboquivari Peak, as clear and close as my hand. I can see a hundred miles, a thousand miles, all the way to Mexico, to the ocean, to Oregon, all the way into every corner of my past. Everything is washed clean and clear.

I came to Tucson like a blind dog on a scent, drawn by remembered terrain—the sandy arroyos and granite cliffs of El Diablo.

I came with nothing but a pregnant dog, a few pots and pans, and the determination to stop, just to stop. I had been trying hard for years in all the proper ways, but something was missing and I was bone-tired from the search. As I did in Diablo Canyon, I simply called off the fight. I found free housing. I took just enough work to get by. And I waited.

Years of hiking in the wilderness have taught me to follow the faintest of trails. Tracking over desert ground this trail has led me back into myself.

When I lose faith I go out to these desert canyons. I hold rocks in my hands and feel their strength. Now on the ridge, I think of my father's words, which it has taken me half my life to understand:

EASTER MORNING
APRIL 12, 1971
LETTER TO ELEANOR FROM BOROKO, NEW GUINEA

When the sun is out our yard dances with butterflies; in the evening a solemn tree frog, bright green with red feet, stares in at my study window; at night I hear the flup flup of a big fruit bat who comes to check on our papayas. It is strange and exotic and gives one a rather detached feeling.

Easter in its larger sense has hardly affected me this year. . . . Rather I find myself thinking in small terms. Individually. We each die continually, almost randomly, one hope at a time. One defeat after another is death enough. But we learn too that no hurt is forever. One recovery at a time, one joy at a time, is resurrection enough.